C000156181

THE HE[
DIARY

Somebunny Loves You

Ken Smith

BLACK & WHITE PUBLISHING

First published 2017
by Black & White Publishing Ltd
Nautical House, 104 Commercial Street
Edinburgh EH6 6NF

1 3 5 7 9 10 8 6 4 2   17 18 19 20

ISBN: 978 1 78530 146 9

Copyright © Ken Smith & Newsquest (Herald & Times) Ltd 2017

The right of Ken Smith & Newsquest (Herald & Times) Ltd to be identified
as the author of this work has been asserted by him in accordance with the
Copyright, Designs and Patents Act 1988.

All rights reserved.
No part of this publication may be reproduced,
stored in a retrieval system, or transmitted in any form, or by any means,
electronic, mechanical, photocopying, recording or otherwise,
without permission in writing from the publisher.

The publisher has made every reasonable effort to contact copyright holders
of images in this book. Any errors are inadvertent and anyone who for any reason
has not been contacted is invited to write to the publisher so that a full
acknowledgment can be made in subsequent editions of this work.

A CIP catalogue record for this book is available from the British Library.

Typeset by Iolaire Typesetting, Newtonmore
Printed and bound by MBM Print, East Kilbride

MIX
Paper from
responsible sources
FSC® C117931

Contents

Introduction

The good thing is that if you're reading this then Donald Trump has not sacrificed us all in a nuclear war. So we can relax and have a bit of a chuckle about Donald.

In fact readers of *The Herald* newspaper had a lot to laugh about in the past year – American golf club owners, Brexit, and Scottish politics of course, but also how to understand women, the daft conversations you hear on buses, explaining your forgetfulness, and the best of Glasgow banter, as well as reminicising about the greats who have recently departed.

The readers' stories are printed in *The Herald*'s daily 'Diary' column, and here are the best of their stories to read once again and thank our lucky stars that we are still here to have a laugh.

1

Only Here for the Banter

Some of the comments you hear on the streets, in shops or pubs are so inspired that they must be passed on so that they are never forgotten. Here are the best *Herald* readers have heard in the past year.

A READER swears to us that he was in his local in Glasgow at the weekend when a woman of a certain age came in to meet her pal who remarked: "That's a lovely coat."

"Thank you," said her pal. "My husband got it for my 40th birthday."

"Well it's certainly worn very well," her pal replied.

GOOD to see the full flavour of a Glasgow conversation coming across on social media. As Glaswegian Ryan Bryceland told pals on Twitter: "Asked the burd in Krispy Kremes for five Nutella doughnuts and she says, 'Have you got any nut allergies?' 'Aye pal, I'm planning suicide by doughnut'."

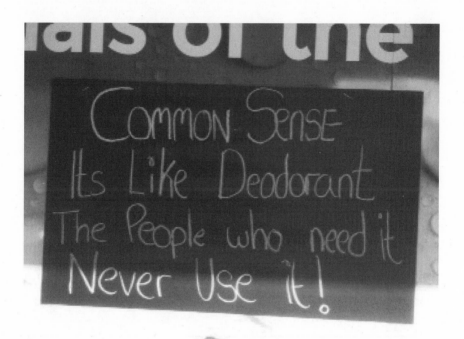

A SOUTHSIDE reader catching a late night bus home from the city centre heard a couple of young women in front of him accusing a mutual friend of being a bit slothful. One girl came up with the memorable assertion: "She's that lazy she only shaves the bits of her legs you can see through her ripped jeans."

A PAISLEY reader swears to us he heard two young women discussing a mutual friend, with one of them claiming the friend was really boring. She emphasised her point by declaring: "Even if she murdered someone, the police still wouldn't describe her as a 'person of interest'."

A READER in the Silverburn shopping centre on Sunday heard a harassed woman tell her pal: "God I hope there's no such thing as reincarnation. I'm way too knackered to do this again."

PEOPLE have mixed views on whether to use automated tills or wait for a real person in the supermarket. A Partick reader tells us: "At least you can still get banter with an actual server. I went in the other day for some toilet rolls, and the normal pack of nine rolls had three free ones. And in addition there were three packs for the price of two, so loaded with 36 rolls I went to the till. "As he swiped the three packages the assistant asked me, 'Curry tonight?'"

BANTER with shop assistants continued. Says a Falkirk reader: "At my local supermarket there was an old chap in front of me who only had six tins of dog food and six cans of lager. The girl on the till looked up and said, 'Whit's this? Is the dug having a party?'"

A FEW folk visited their local council dumps at the weekend. Said Davie Adams in Knightswood: "I went up to my local re-cycling centre yesterday and sought advice from one of the attendants as to where I might place an old mirror - in the furniture bay or the household skip. His instant reply was, 'Aye, pit it in wi' the furniture if ye like, but if ye've nae problems wi' thon seven years bad luck s***e, just pit it in the skip'."

A TRUE word from a colleague who remarks to us: "My mate has closed down his Facebook account.
　"We won't see his likes again."

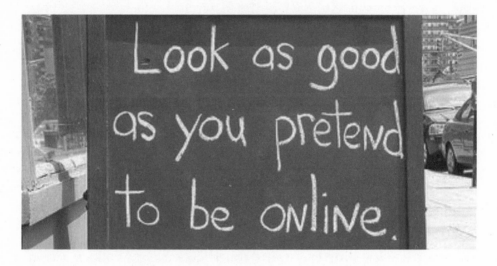

AND a chap in an Ayrshire golf club the other week was heard to argue: "My children had the cheek to say I need to go to anger management classes. I told them I didn't need anger management, I just needed people to stop irritating me."

STV claimed that Canadian singer Justin Bieber popped into a branch of the Blue Lagoon chip shop chain for a haggis supper and a can of Irn-Bru after his show at Glasgow's Hydro. They stated that he handed over £20.
　We like an unimpressed Colin Bell on social media who

commented: "Justin Bieber comes to Glasgow and pays £20 for a haggis supper and a can of Irn-Bru? They saw you coming, mate. Absolutely stitched up."

COMPANIES like to engage with customers on social media, so we like the chap who contacted Tesco and asked: "Would I be able to access your CCTV? Unfortunately I was robbed at your Cardiff store today."

Tesco replied: "We would not give out that information to you personally. You would have to raise it with the police."

Which is just what he wanted as he replied: "I phoned the police but they said Tesco charging you £17 for Gillette blades was not robbery."

THE Bank of England has issued its first plastic fivers, and a number of charities have suggested that people make their first such five-pound note memorable by donating it to charity. Not everyone got the memo it seems. A reader on the bus into Glasgow heard a young chap tell his mate: "Got my first new plastic fiver yesterday. I had to roll it up and use it as a spoon for my yoghurt."

A GLASGOW reader swears to us he was in a trendy coffee shop in the city when the barista behind the counter asked the chap behind him in the queue: "Would you like to try our new Old Paradise Street blend, with hints of bittersweet chocolate?" "Listen pal," replied the customer. "All I want is something that will keep me awake and hopefully not hit any of my workmates."

WE would never condone violence, but football fans were heatedly debating the Hibs v Morton game and the claim by Hibs manager Neil Lennon that shaven-headed, Maryhill-born Morton manager Jim Duffy challenged him to a square-go.

There were even polls on who would win such an exchange with perhaps the most colourful description was the fan who declared: "Jim Duffy would have thrown him about like a wet trackie."

A GLASGOW reader swears to us he was in his local at the weekend where a chap with "Love" and "Hate" tattooed on his knuckles said he had got a quote to have them removed but it was very expensive. When he asked if there was a cheaper alternative the tattoo remover said: "You could get a job in a milliners, and I'll simply change the final 'E' to an 'S'."

READER Drew Fleming passes on: "A friend recently met an ex-colleague who had been suffering from the effects of flu symptoms that have been all the rage. On enquiring how he was feeling, the reply was, 'I feel rather like the wee man I saw going into the bookies - a little better!'"

A MILNGAVIE reader who has been trying to find someone to repair the family's old grandfather clock says he still remembers when it broke down 50 years ago when he was just a lad. He remembers the old chap who came to repair it who opened up the back and announced in a fake German accent: "Ve half vays of making you toc!" Our reader wonders how often he came out with that line in his career.

COMMENTS that only work in Scotland, we suspect. David Leask reported in Saturday's *Herald* that John Devlin, the majority shareholder in Mortons Rolls, had been struck off by the Institute of Chartered Accounts Scotland due to misconduct. "Well fired," commented a *Herald* reader.

A GLASGOW reader buying a sandwich in a city centre coffee shop thought the reply was inspired when a woman in the queue was accused by her pal of being difficult to get hold of.

"I don't agree with that," she replied. "I never have my fax machine switched off."

WE noticed that a colleague who likes to interrupt us is on a day off. Good stuff.

But then the phone rings, and he's on the line to tell us: "I'm looking out my tenement window and there's a neighbour struggling to hang out his washing, and he's pointing at me and swearing.

"I'm going to take him down a peg or two."

GLASGOW comedian Scott Agnew passes on: "Old boy in Tesco to checkout boy, 'There'll be nae self service for me son - too bliddy complicated. And just you pack they bags fur us, cheers'.

"He then steps back, produces a smartphone, and skelps £20 away on his Skybet app."

CONGRATULATIONS on Paisley making it to the shortlist for the UK's City of Culture, 2021. We liked the reaction of one reader of an English newspaper reporting the shortlist who commented: "I spent nine joyous years working in Paisley. Great town, great people, great fun. Following St Mirren is a life-long exercise in hope over experience. OK, broadcaster Andrew Neil is from there, as is banker Fred 'The Shred' Goodwin, but every town has its low-lifes."

NOT everyone's an optimist in Glasgow. A Shawlands reader heard a young woman on his bus yesterday tell her pal: "I swear I can make just about anything happen simply by hoping it won't."

SOMETIMES we feel the need to pass on messages from social media. As a Pete Bradley commented the other day: "Picked up my mum, steaming, and she said, 'Can we get chips?' to which I replied, 'No. We have some in the freezer'. Been waiting years to say that'."

SHAME sat nav means we no longer ask for directions. Andy Gallagher in Langside once set himself up for a Glasgow comic when he stopped his car in Highburgh Road in Hyndland and asked a passing pedestrian how he could get to Jordanhill College.

"Without hesitation, he told me, 'You'll need your Highers son'."

A FEW folk have been saying that there seems to be a few more folk begging on the city centre streets in Glasgow than there used to be.

A reader once told us that on Great Western Road he overheard a chap telling someone who stopped him for change: "Why don't you sell *The Big Issue*?" The mendicant replied: "I regard this as more of a challenge." It got him a quid.

A LAID-BACK, long-haired surfer type from San Diego, California has been sitting in Glasgow's Buchanan Street selling friendship bracelets he makes with a sign beside him stating "Handmade bracelets by this handsome guy".

Deedee Cuddihy chatted with him and he revealed that, while he liked Glasgow, people frequently stopped and asked him: "Is the 'handsome guy' away for his lunch break?"

OUR story about furniture left out for the binmen reminds David Miller in Milngavie: "Comedian Lex McLean told the story of how he was called into the burroo to explain why he had been seen selling firewood in Dumbarton Road. 'Selling firewood?' he exclaimed. 'I was flitting!'"

OH, to be back in Glasgow. Returning expat Andrew Foster, now domiciled in Ontario, tells us: "Enjoying being back to familiar things.

"Ticket machine wouldn't work for me at Central Station this morning, and I grumped to the ticket man that it didn't like me.

"'Lucky ye're no' married to it, then', came back the compassionate reply."

MORE on street traders, as Andy Cumming recalls: "I once heard a guy selling plants at the Barras, 'Get yer bedding plants here. Take them home and let them die in the privacy of your own home'."

AH the Glasgow banter. John Dunlop from Bearsden tells us: "During the recent demolition of a derelict community centre in Easterhouse, and with tongue heavily planted in cheek, I asked the contractor what he was going to do about the resident rats whose house he was taking away. Quick as a flash came the reply, 'It's OK - we're re-homing them in Pollok'."

MORE on street traders as musician Jimmie Macgregor recounts: "My mother, Annie Macgregor, loved the Barras and said that in her time it was the best cabaret in town. She used to tell of two elderly friends who ran adjacent fruit stalls. The first, obviously bored with the usual selling spiel, would roar, 'Perrs, a pun. Aipples, a hauf pun. Bananas each'. Her colleague simply shouted, 'Same as Mary'."

STREET traders continued. Says Eddie Boyle in Ontario: "Some wee wummin asked the guy in the Barras selling sheets and blankets in the sixties if the eiderdown bedspread was big enough for a double bed. He replied, 'Missus, it's big enough to cover your bed, go alang the flerr for a carpet, and up the windae for curtains'."

WE'VE mentioned a few withering put-downs. Douglas McIntyre adds: "Our family's old Aunty Polly occasionally spoke of a girl she was friendly with back in her youth. She would tell us, 'She was so ugly that even the tide widnae take her oot!'"

2

I Belong to Glasgow

It's true that *The Herald* covers the whole of Scotland but at its beating heart is the industrial city of Glasgow. Here are some of the city's stories, many of which we suspect would not happen elsewhere.

A READER passing the Rufus T Firefly bar in Hope Street was much taken with the chalk-board outside which carried the message: "To the guy who keeps coming in to do a wee jobby without buying anything, then pretends to be on his phone on the road oot to avoid eye contact - Hiya Pal!"

SO what's been happening on the streets of Glasgow? Well Amy Neil explained on social media: "Just seen a drunk woman get knocked down in Glasgow, then two seconds later stand up and shout, 'It's awrite - I stayed loose.' Is this for real?"

A READER says he had to laugh when he heard a woman in a coffee shop in Glasgow at the weekend tell her pals: "My pain threshold is very low - like that of a man's."

A GLASGOW reader passes on a comment from his mate in the pub at the weekend when how supportive our parents were was discussed. "When I was growing up," said his pal, "my mum was always saying, 'You can do it!' "Just like when I was asking who was making the tea."

ARE you, like us, shaking your head when you meet people ostentatiously wearing these Fitbits around their wrists that measures the number of steps they take? We pass on the pure daftness of comedy writer Iain Connell, who comments: "There's a garage in Possil that'll add 500 miles to your Fitbit for a tenner."

SUGGESTIONS have been made that the old Scottish staple, the plain loaf, might be on its way out due to falling demand. It reminds us of actor Alex Norton's tale of the Glasgow punter who dreamed that the winner of the Derby had something to do with bread, so his heart missed a beat when he saw one of the horses was called Mother's Pride. Putting all his cash on it, he went in to the bookie's after, only to be told his horse came last. "It canny have. Ah dreamed it had something to do with bread."

"Well," said the bookie's clerk. "It wiz won by some big ootsider."

TALK of the council spending millions to tart up Byres Road in the West End reminds us of conversations that you only seem to hear there. We recall the woman meeting friends for cocktails in a Byres Road bar who said she had come off her bike because of a huge pot hole, then added: "Fortunately, I remembered my ballet training, and did a beautiful arabesque into the bushes."

NOT been in the taxi queue late at night at Central Station for a while, which is a shame as you meet all human life there. A Pollokshields reader who was there at the weekend heard the perfect, barbed apology, when the young woman in front of him told her pal: "I'm sorry if you were offended when I called you an idiot.

"I honestly thought you already knew."

YOU can't beat the generosity of Glaswegians. A worker at Glasgow's great Prince and Princess of Wales Hospice tells us: "A kind soul recently donated a toastie maker, still in the box, to one of our shops in Glasgow. It was only when the box was opened that the shop assistant realised an old toastie maker had been donated in the box of a new one. And inside the toastie maker? A very old and very mouldy cheese toastie.

"Someone out there has been waiting a long time for their savoury snack."

A READER tells us of being on the Subway when two strangers got into a conversation about how the white line on the platform to keep passengers back from the edge is lighter at the points where the doors open.

Both chaps got off to check, and were not quick enough to get back on board before the doors closed. Particularly agitated was the wife of one of them who was now waving frantically at the window while travelling on the Subway without her husband.

WE spot a young woman in Buchanan Street who is wearing striped trousers that make her look like a pirate. We say nothing as we are reminded of Glasgow author Deedee Cuddihy's book *The Wee Guide To Scottish Women* in which she says she was sporting a pair of brand-new sailor-style trousers in Argyle Street when she passed some young girls who remarked: "Shiver me timbers." Says Deedee: "I consigned the trendy trews to the back of the wardrobe after that, never to be worn again."

JUST a slice of modern life: Robert Thompson in Bearsden tells us: "I was travelling on the 60 bus along Maryhill Road last week when a lady came on in her housecoat, nightie and slippers. She told the driver she was only coming on to collect a copy of the free paper before she got back off again."

GLASGOW stand-up Janey Godley marked International Women's Day on social media with the story: "This is what being a woman feels like. Glasgow Tube. Ticket machine never worked so the man behind the counter sighed and said 'Women' and told me I was doing it wrong and shouted instructions at me doing hand signals at my head like I was mentally ill.

"A man came along and the next machine never worked either, and the man came out and they discussed why it never worked. This was two days ago."

THE *Evening Times* reported that Glasgow City Council has asked the Scottish Government to take over the running of the Clyde Tunnel because of worries about future repair costs.

It reminds us of when the tunnel was built and the tunnellers often suffered from compressed air sickness which made them look as though they were drunk.

It got so bad that they were given badges which explained they were staggering because of their work in the tunnel.

Police in Govan however got fed up with so many weekend imbibers who had copies of the badges in the hope it would stop them from being barred from pubs.

THE Glasgow International Comedy Festival starts this week,

and we liked the observation by Hebridean Carina MacLeod, appearing at Yes Bar this Saturday, who was asked in an interview what her best experience of Glasgow has been.

She replied: "Waking up at a party when I was 17, under the stairs on a dog blanket and not knowing anyone. That was an eye opener for any Hebridean."

A GLASGOW reader was in his local supermarket when he noticed that even the gents' toilet had a baby-changing shelf that you could fold down.

He just passes on the fact that even that was not free of graffiti as someone had neatly written on it "Place sacrifice here".

ACTOR and writer Greg Hemphill announced the new series of *Still Game* begins filming next week and urged folk to give them a shout if they see them out on the street.

TV producer Michael McAvoy replied to Greg: "I miss the times when any camera crew in Glasgow (no matter how small) was presumed to be *Taggart* and folk shouted, 'There's been a murder!'"

JOKES that only work in Glasgow, continued. Says Andy Bollen: "I bumped into Theresa May, Donald Trump and Vladimir Putin in Maryhill. They were looking for the G20 Summit. I'll get my coat."

A COMMUTER coming out of Queen Street Station noticed a large number of fag ends stuck into the crevices between the bricks on a wall, giving almost a modern art effect, with the brown and white of the ciggies sticking out at different angles in contrast to the colour of the bricks.

Her reverie was broken by a passer-by who explained: "It's to avoid getting a fine for flinging them on the grun."

THAT great Trongate music pub Maggie May's has been relaunched after a £400,000 refurbishment by new owners Stephen White and Oli Norman. A fan of Rod Stewart, who wrote the song Maggie May, told us: "If I ever bump into Rod I'm going to tell him that 'The morning sun when it's in your face, really shows your age' is not a great chat-up line."

WE are always intrigued about the differences between Edinburgh and Glasgow, and learn a new one from the armed forces charity SSAFA, which is holding its Big Brew Up next month when folk hold tea parties to raise funds for service personnel families in need.

It has surveyed what people dunk in their tea, and in Edinburgh teacakes make the top 10. In Glasgow, nothing that posh makes the list. Instead the Glasgow list includes something not mentioned in Edinburgh - crisps.

SINGER Jimmie Macgregor recalls a visit to Glasgow's Barras: "There was a gent selling a complicated metal contraption, claiming that you could not fail to charm your companion as you glided around the dance floor, by singing a romantic ballad through the kazoo which was attached to your nose.

"Never really worked for me."

STREET traders continued. Says John Parker in Glasgow's West End: "My wife and I were walking through the Barras a few years ago and heard a DVD salesman espousing the positives of a Barras' DVD. 'Not one film, not two films, but three films on wan disc - just the way Disney disnae do them'."

MEANWHILE in America, the Baltimore weekly newspaper, *City Paper*, has carried an article on the similarities between the city and Glasgow. The article mentions the film *Braveheart* and memorably explains: "The movie is a hell of a good time, and, historically, frothing with what in Scotland they call 'pish'."

READER William Hill in Bishopton, Renfrewshire, takes us down memory lane as he recalls the Govan street market in its 50s heyday when a confectionary stall-holder would shout out to passing female shoppers: "Hurry hurry, Mrs Murray", or "Two for a fiver, Mrs McIver". Says William: "He would also shout at women of his age who passed his stall, 'Ah remember you - you used to go to the Barrowland dancing'. Most women had a quiet smile to themselves and walked on until one woman stopped, looked him up and down, and said, 'Aye that's right, ah remember you. I see you're still wearing the same jaiket'.

"For once the stallholder was speechless."

WE turn to social media for an insight into what's happening in Glasgow, and Richard Laird comments: "Woman walking down Sauchiehall Street smoking from a cigarette holder. The once proud working class city of Glasgow has gone full Gatsby."

STEVEN Camley's cartoon of the soup tin in *The Herald* reminded Bruce Henderson in Straiton, Ayrshire: "In the 1950s, we celebrated our engagement at Reo Stakis's newly opened Ca'Dora Restaurant in Union Street to enjoy his French menu. "We both ordered Creme de Pompador as a starter. As the Glaswegian waitress kicked open the kitchen door, she shouted: 'Two toma'a soups'."

3

Living in Weans' World

People will claim that Scots love nothing better than a drink or football. Not true! Scots always have a soft spot for the weans, even if they do drive us demented.

A BEARSDEN reader emails us: "I was so distracted in the kitchen at the weekend that I asked my dog to hand me something. To be fair, he gave me the same blank stare my children would have."

A HILLHEAD reader tells us her friend is at loggerheads with her teenage daughter and has stopped washing her daughter's clothes until she helps more around the house.

"At the rate she goes through outfits," says the mother, "she'll be down to wearing Hallowe'en costumes by next week."

THE tricky subject of commenting on a baby who is lacking in the looks department reminds retired Dundee health visitor Christine Docherty: "I remember asking my mentor health visitor jokingly what you said when you looked in the pram on the visit and the baby was 'not bonny' (a well used Dundonian expression). She reassured me that the best response was to say, 'Nice pram'. Worked everytime!"

SAD news that the great West End toyshop The Sentry Box, just off Byres Road, is to close. That'll teach us to use the internet so much. Anyway, it reminds us of the harassed mother, fed up hearing her childless friends go on about their fabulous spa weekends, telling them: "The nearest I get to a spa is when the wean drives his toy truck over my back."

A WEST End reader tells us: "A woman in my local coffee shop at the weekend was telling her pals, 'You can never tell a woman that her baby is ugly, so a polite way to do it is to tell her that it looks just like her husband'."

A READER tells us the young woman on the train into Glasgow

yesterday morning was telling her pal: "I spent the weekend looking after my sister's kids.

"I mean, that's got to be worth a kidney if I ever need one."

A READER heard a toper in a Glasgow pub at the weekend tell his pals: "The kids were having a big noisy argument about which one was my favourite.

"The family dog just gave me a knowing look, and I quietly slipped him a biscuit."

MORE views on parenting, as a Jordanhill teacher tells us: "My children are very optimistic - every glass they leave lying around the house is half full."

ANDREW McMillan from Renfrew was in his local Lidl supermarket when he heard a wee girl about seven ask her gran if she could get an ice cream. Says Andrew: "Her gran answered, 'Well, if you eat all your dinner I'll take you to the ice cream parlour'. But the girl insisted, 'I want an ice cream from here'.

"Her gran told her, 'Well, I want Gerard Butler, but he's unavailable. We can't always get what we want'."

SAYS John Bannerman in Kilmaurs: "At the meeting of the Irvine Meadow Supporters Club, the speaker told of a player from Renfrewshire, who was an identical twin, and was once pushed with his brother in Paisley in his pram-for-two by their doting mother. A kindly shopper stopped to admire the bonny boys and asked, 'My goodness, they are so alike. How do you tell them apart?' "'Balls', the mother replied. As the woman looked a bit shocked, the mother added, 'This one bawls aw moarnin, and when HE stops, the ither yin starts'."

PARENTING teenagers, continued. A Merrylee father tells us: "My son has just passed his driving test and on Saturday he texted me, 'Can I borrow the car later?' I thought I was quite clever when I texted back, 'Of course you can! But that's not how you spell 'wash'."

MODERN-DAY parenting continued. A Renfrewshire reader emails: "My five-year-old daughter has threatened not to talk to me for the rest of the day. I'm a quarter offended, and three-quarters wishing she sticks to her word."

TODAY'S piece of whimsy comes from Craig Deeley who says: "Necessity is the mother of Invention. And there are lots more people in our family with stupid names."

OUR mentions of parenting skills brings a response from a Hillhead reader who says, 'If a four-year-old says, 'I'm scared there's a monster living under my bed,' don't reply, 'Oh, that's where he's been hiding'.
   "I know that now."

ROUKEN Glen Park in East Renfrewshire has been voted Britain's Best Park in a poll carried out by the charity Fields In Trust.

It's a lovely park - even has its own waterfall. We remember a reader telling us he was there one summer's evening when an excitable toddler asked her mum: "Can we go to the waterfall?" But the mother answered sorrowfully: "No darling. I'm so sorry, we can't. They switch it off at night."

AFTER recent observations about parenting in the Diary, an Edinburgh reader emails to tell us: "Basically parenting consists of telling your children to eat more fruit, then later telling them to stop eating all the fruit."

A READER emails with the observation: "Dads. If it's your own children, it's called staying in, not babysitting."

A YOUNG father phones to tell us: "Now that I have my own kids I realise old sayings should be rewritten. Such as, 'If it ain't broke, then my kids haven't played with it yet'."

A SOUTHSIDE reader who sneaked out from the festive fun at home to have a pint said he overheard some young chaps at the bar discussing the merits of having children. One father of young kids put in his tuppence worth by stating: "You have to ask yourself before you do, are you willing to watch the same Disney film on a permanent loop for the next four years of your life?"

A PARTICK reader hears a chap in the pub at the weekend declare to his pals: "I have this constant fear that one of my children will become a world-famous artist, and I'll sit there thinking of the millions of pounds worth of art I've thrown in the bin."

BRINGING up children, continued. A reader confesses to us: "Based on the things my children will and won't eat, my cooking is apparently worse than a Polo Mint found on the floor with dog hair on it."

ANOTHER take on raising children as a Dumbarton reader tells us: "My younger son says he can't do his sums at school but give him a slice of pepperoni pizza and he can tell you instantly if you've given his brother a slice with more bits of pepperoni."

NICE day for getting out yesterday. Says Bruce Skivington: "While out this morning I noticed aggressive-looking dogs wearing yellow coats with the logo, 'I need space' to warn people. Do you know where you can get these coats for grandchildren?"

OUR tales about the good points and bad points of having children brings forth an email from a Jordanhill reader: "A definite benefit of having kids is how you're able to use them as an excuse to suddenly cancel things at the last minute you don't want to go to."

A READER tells us a friend has just gone back to work after paternity leave. So our reader asked him how it had been, and although he said fine, he did add that two weeks was not the right amount of time off. "Did you want longer?" asked our reader. "No, shorter," he replied.

PARENTING continued. A Southside reader says she can't understand why people complain about their teenage children not keeping their rooms tidy. She tells us: "I only have to tell my son that I'm going up to clean his room as I love snooping through his stuff, and before you know it, he's up there doing it himself."

WE mentioned bad parenting techniques and a Stirling reader tells us: "My son is petrified of thunder. I told him that was ridiculous - it's the lightning that will kill you not the thunder."

THE joys of parenting. A Hyndland reader tells us: "Apparently I ruined my four-year-old's entire life by using the wrong shade of yellow when helping him paint the sun."

BRINGING up children continued. A Shawlands mother says

she read that young children can grow an average of two inches a year. She says it's a shame though that it occurs within a day of buying them new clothes.

A HILLHEAD reader tells us his son asked for two toys to be bought for him at the weekend, but dad said it was pointless as he could only concentrate with one at a time, so he could choose only one.

On Monday the lad came home from school with two pieces of homework to do and tried to argue with his father that it was pointless doing two as he could only concentrate on one.

A NEWTON Mearns reader contacts us to ask: "Why is it when I go to the supermarket and text my teenage daughter to ask her if she needs anything, I get no reply. Then, half an hour later, just as I'm going through the checkout, she texts me with a list of things she wants?"

TODAY'S piece of daftness comes from an Ayr reader who says: "Was out washing the car at the weekend with my son.

"Wife says I should use a chamois next time."

GETTING old continued. Says a reader in Knightswood: "I was telling my granddaughter that when Neil Armstrong became the first man to walk on the moon there were precisely five pictures taken of him on the surface. And then I asked her, 'So why is it you've had to take 50 pictures of yourself simply because you've had your eyebrows done?'"

A FALKIRK reader tells us her son sat down at the dinner table and picked up a chicken leg with his fingers. "Did you wash your hands?" she asked him. "No," he replied.

"Why not?" she asked, not unreasonably. "I don't want the chicken to taste of soap," he replied.

A READER heard a mother moan to her pals in a Glasgow coffee shop: " I took all my kids' electronic devices away so we could spend some quality time together. Turns out they are really terrible to be around so I gave them their stuff back."

READERS have been pondering children's names after Tory MP Jacob Rees-Mogg named his sixth child Sixtus Dominic Boniface Christopher. Reader John Delaney in Lochwinnoch tells us: "There was a family at my wife's school with four sons. Their fifth child was born a girl, and the parents called her 'Chanel Number 5'."

TALKING of fathers, an Ayrshire reader tells us one of his golf-club members announced at the weekend: "My lad asked me for one of those fidget spinner things. I told him I had something bigger and better for him to try - and took him out to the lawnmower."

And another father says he was on the computer at home when his little son came over and asked him what game he was playing. Says dad: "I told him I was paying bills. He asked me if I was winning. I had to tell him that sadly no, I wasn't."

AS folk make their plans for the summer holidays, a Bearsden reader tells us: "Hubbie and I wanted to go back to Majorca but our teenage children moaned that they wanted to try something new.

"So I showed them where the vacuum cleaner and the washing machine were kept."

RAISING children, continued. A Bearsden reader was in the lounge with his daughter while his wife and son were in the kitchen.

He suddenly heard a loud crash, and wondered aloud who had dropped something.

"Mum," said his daughter.

"How do you know?" he asked.

"She didn't say anything," replied daughter.

A MILNGAVIE reader tells us she returned home after a bracing walk in the country and asked her daughter what her favourite season was. Her daughter merely replied: "The second season of Game of Thrones."

BRINGING up teenagers, continued. Says Elizabeth Hackett: "I'd only want to be a teenager again so that when someone has just finished lecturing me, I can pull off my headphones and say 'What?'"

MODERN parenting continued. A Jordanhill reader tells us her friend, who is the mother of a young one, confessed to her: "Was it bad of me to smile when my child stood on a piece of Lego in his bare feet hours after I'd been nagging him to pick all the pieces up?"

TOUGH being a parent. A Partick reader was in his local supermarket where he heard a mother shout at her child: "No!" The young lad looked at her and said in a hurt tone: "But I didn't ask for anything."

"You looked as if you were about to," she replied.

A DARNLEY reader continues our parenting theme by explaining: "When I say, 'Time to get in the car', my five-year-old somehow hears, 'Time to start looking for that toy we've not seen for over a year'."

VERBAL misunderstandings continued. Says Margaret Thomson: "Many years ago, I was seeing my company of Life Boys out after an evening meeting. I spotted a pair of sandshoes and called after the boys. One wee lad came back, looked at the shoes and said, 'They're mashoos'. So I told him to take them. 'No miss, they're mashoos!' I was about to lose it when he continued, 'They're Mashoo Brown's'."

A CLARKSTON reader says she is feeling very old after her young son asked her what happened to dinosaurs. When she told him that they had all died off, he asked her: "Why did you let them die?"

A HYNDLAND reader tells us: "Fifteen years ago I won a prize in the university's debating team. Who knew I would use these skills to try to convince my seven-year-old that the shape of the pasta doesn't change its taste."

A LENZIE reader emails to say: "I did not see many kids out playing with new footballs after Christmas. My mother always remembered a mate of mine coming to the door and asking if I was coming out to play when I was a youngster. When she said I had a cold and was staying in, he asked if my football could come out to play."

4

It Gets Our Vote

There's no denying it has been some year for politics. Serious stuff of course, but amongst all the doom and gloom, a smile or two did appear.

WE liked the honesty of Scots Lib Dems' leader Willie Rennie discussing cannabis on Radio Scotland when he explained he used it at university. "Do you still use it now Willie?" he was asked.

"It might look like it, but I don't," he replied.

AND the claim that the Labour Party manifesto is reminiscent of the seventies was being discussed in a Glasgow pub yesterday. One toper claimed: "When I was a nipper in the seventies, my father was a shop steward. He would begin every bedtime story, 'Once upon a time and a half.'"

DONALD Trump's 100 days in office appear to have been commemorated at the Ubiquitous Chip's wee bar in Glasgow's Ashton Lane, where reader John Sim from Dumbarton notices in the cocktail list a drink called a "Letter to America". Below the title is the explanation: "Yer Maw Was An Immigrant, Ya Absolute Roaster".

THE Tories are keen on voter ID at elections, although this would disenfranchise those with no passport or driving licence. It reminds us of the Glasgow polling station at a previous election where the official, with pen and ruler poised to score a voter off the list, asked a chap where he lived.

The official was nonplussed by the reply: "Roon the corner fae the swing park."

FORMER Tory Minister Iain Duncan Smith told the BBC's *Today* programme yesterday the government's objective in the Brexit negotiations was to leave the European Union. Glad he

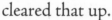

cleared that up.

We cannot forget our colleague David Leask telling us: "The only time I saw IDS in Glasgow, a lass with a bald wean yelled, 'Oi Tory boy! See the last time you were here!' and pointed in her pram."

GLASGOW comedian Frankie Boyle has been commenting on Donald Trump wanting Mexico to pay for a wall being built between that country and America. Said Frankie: "To be fair, I managed to get my neighbour to build a wall and pay for it, and all it cost me was the price of a thong to sunbathe in."

IT'S just over three months to the local council elections in Scotland, and we remember years ago a Glasgow Labour MP complaining about the lack of help he got in his election campaign from local councillors. As he put it: "It's funny how some councillors can't climb a flight of stairs in a tenement to deliver a leaflet, but can happily skip up a flight of stairs to a plane if a foreign trip is in the offing."

CAMPAIGNING in Edinburgh South West, Tory candidate Miles Briggs was surprised when the occupant rushed to get a camera and asked to take his picture.

When Miles asked why, the man replied, "Because I thought Tories were extinct." Worse still, the awkward encounter was being recorded by the BBC for a profile of the seat.

WESTERN Isles MP Angus MacNeil was chastised by the Speaker for chewing gum in the Commons. As John Bercow chided: "I have great aspirations for you to be a statesman. But I think your apprenticeship still has some distance to travel."

Angus has always been a rebel. We recall when the *Oban Times* reported that at a Camanachd Cup final a friend of Angus found himself at the back of a long queue for the toilet. Said the *Times*: "Along came Angus, who quickly assessed the waiting time would be too long. He lifted his friend off the ground, all 13 stone of him, and carried him past the queue, shouting, 'Prostate emergency - clear the way, please'. "The Fort William supporter was relieved to find himself at the head of the queue and so, of course, was Angus."

STV Holyrood editor Colin Mackay, hosting the Politician of the Year awards in Edinburgh last night, couldn't help having a go at presidential candidate Donald Trump. Said Colin: "You know if you go to Turnberry, you'll see the giant portrait of Trump there. His hands seem to follow you around the room."

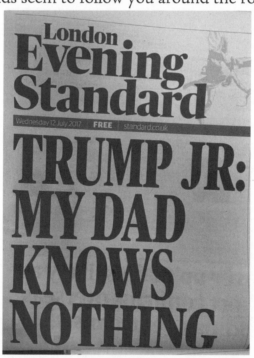

THE Herald reported that Professor Stephen Hawking has called for Jeremy Corbyn to stand down as Labour leader, claiming he is a "disaster" for the party.

Naturally we turn to social media for a paranoid reaction where someone posted: "Who knows if it is Hawking who said that? For all we know MI5 could have hacked his machine. Corbyn terrifies the establishment, they will stop at nothing to remove him."

HARD to believe there was some opposition to the Scottish government's scheme to give a baby box full of essentials to new babies, which could also be used as a cot. As Bruce Skivington comments: "It is an excellent idea, the government giving every baby a cardboard box to sleep in.

"If Brexit goes ahead we shall all be sleeping in cardboard boxes."

THE Herald's archive picture the other day of Celtic's Jock Stein and Rangers' Willie Henderson meeting Prime Minister Harold Wilson in Glasgow reminds Willie of that day. He tells us: "I asked him about the pipe he always had in his hand. He said he carried it in case any journalist asked an awkward question. He would then take a minute to fill it with tobacco which gave him time to think of a good answer."

FORMER Scots Secretary Malcolm Rifkind, who has just published his autobiography, is speaking at the Wigtown Book Festival at the end of the month. It reminds us of Sir Malcolm, when he was Foreign Secretary, telling the yarn about the British minister speaking in Moscow at the height of the Cold War, who declared in a speech: "The spirit is willing, but the flesh is weak."

He was surprised later to see the speech translated into Russian as: "We have lots of vodka, but we're rather short of meat."

THE *Herald* archive photograph of Margaret Thatcher on her first trip to Scotland as prime minister reminds my old colleague Jack Webster of flying up to Edinburgh with Maggie and husband Denis that day, which he wrote about in his book *A Final Grain of Truth*. Said Jack: "Denis, sitting on my left with gin and tonic, was a funny man. He told the story of sitting down in an empty rail carriage, and only then noticing that the carriage was reserved for the annual outing of a mental institution. Sure enough, they were soon crowding around him and the superintendent began a head count. 'One, two, three, four', then came to Denis. 'Who are you?' she asked.

"Denis said, 'I'm the husband of the prime minister'. The superintendent continued, 'Five, six, seven'."

ANOTHER American phones to give us their views on the presidential elections. She tells us: "Last year our biggest argument was whether a dress pictured online by a Scottish couple was blue and black or whether it was white and gold. This year we're wondering whether the human race will destroy itself because we voted in an unstable president."

SOCIAL media can be such fun. A UKIP follower on Twitter wrote the other day: "We are a western Christian country. If people are offended by Christmas I'll personally drive them to the airport."

Within minutes someone replied: "Hi. I'm offended by Christmas and I'm flying out of Luton on Thursday. Pick me up about 10.15am?"

OH, what a lark. BBC Scotland is frequently accused of being biased, so when morning radio presenter Gary Robertson asked on social media: "Driverless cars likely to be on UK roads by end of the decade. Who is at fault if they crash?" it was perhaps inevitable that a Cliff McCabe would reply ironically: "My guess is the SNP, Gary. Is there a prize in this competition?"

DAVE McFarlane in Motherwell opines: "How bad a politician must Hillary Clinton be to lose to Donald Trump for goodness sake? She's the Scottish football team of politics."

WHAT happens when Trump takes over in the White House? A forlorn hope from Mark Simpson who asks: "Can Obama not just turn the telly up really loud and pretend he didn't hear the doorbell?"

AND we don't think the chap was serious who wrote to the Facebook page of Mr Trump's golf course in Aberdeenshire: "With Donald's recent appointment as president of the United States, does that mean his Saturday shift behind the bar is available? Just thought I'd ask for a mate."

TOP Tory Michael Heseltine is quoted by the BBC denying that he had choked to death his mother's Alsatian dog many years ago. What strange times we live in. A Better Together supporter - they still exist apparently - emails us: "As Heseltine denies choking a dog called Kim, police to investigate rumours of people in Scotland flogging a dead horse called Indyref2."

DAVE Biggart in Kilmalcolm says: "The article in *The Herald* about Pravda setting up an Edinburgh office reminded me of the headline in the infamous Russian newspaper when President Khrushchev was holding talks with President Kennedy at the time of the Cuban missile crisis.

"It read, 'In his first ever game of golf, President Khrushchev came second. President Kennedy came next to last."

WE realise it was First Minister's Questions at the Scottish

Parliament yesterday and we turn to social media to see if we missed anything. One observer wrote: "Ruth made some considered, perceptive points, Kezia criticised the Tories, and folk sat up and noticed Willie.

"Only joking."

WITH all this Brexit stuff, we shouldn't forget what Donald Trump is up to in America. A reader in the States explains: "As he starts to cut environmental legislation put in place by Obama, Donald Trump says the hole in the ozone layer can be covered by simply combing some over from the side."

IT seems Nicola Sturgeon has not won round everyone in England. Says reader Jim Gordon: "A friend 'down south' advised me of a new term in the golf lexicon. It's 'a Sturgeon' - apparently it means 'an awkward little five-footer'.

THE Herald archive picture of Prime Minister Harold Wilson in Glasgow reminds Donald Gillies of being in the city centre at the time of the visit. "Wilson emerged from a car to enter an office in St Vincent Street. A group of Rangers fans was passing and Wilson, trying to be the man of the people, addressed them cheerily, 'Ah off to win the cup?' Unbeknownst to him, Rangers had recently been knocked out the cup by Hearts, so he looked somewhat shaken when one of the fans replied, 'Beat it, Fatty!'"

BIG golf news yesterday was the very posh Muirfield Golf Club taking a second vote, and this time agreeing to allow women members. As reader Kenny Gillies tells us: "I can't help noticing that there has been no criticism of the Honourable Company of Edinburgh Golfers for holding another referendum on allowing women to become members at Muirfield just 10 months after the last vote."

BUDGET yesterday, so we turn to writer David Schneider to explain it to us: "Chancellor Philip Hammond said in his speech, 'We are the party of the NHS'.

"In other news, lions are the health and safety executive for antelopes."

TALKING about Trump, a reader in America emails: "The Justice Department asked the FBI if the claim that Trump's phone had been tapped was true or not. The director of the FBI replied, 'The claim President Trump made to his son-in-law in a phone call to his private apartment at 11.19am last Monday has no basis in fact'."

THE latest Trump news was that he played a round of golf with top Irish player Rory McIlroy the other day. Some folk were upset Rory played with the president, and Belfast comedian Tim McGarry suggested: "Hint to Rory McIlroy - next time Donald Trump asks you to play golf, tell him you're a refugee from a country renowned for terrorism."

CONGRATULATIONS on satirical magazine *Private Eye*

recording its best sales figures. The mag has for years used the euphemism "Ugandan affairs" when referring to sex. As Margaret Thatcher's biographer Charles Moore once observed: "She could not understand jokes, and had no clue what the reference to 'Ugandan affairs' meant in relation to Cecil Parkinson's affair with Sarah Keays. 'I know it's untrue', she exclaimed. 'He's never been to Africa'."

COMMONS Speaker John Bercow is getting much praise for declaring that he doesn't think Donald Trump deserves an invitation to address Parliament. We just hope his power to forecast the future has improved since he was Tory parliamentary candidate in Motherwell in the 1980s and declared on his election leaflet: "Conservatives recognise the crucial importance of the Scottish steel industry. Ravenscraig is now profitable and there is no question of it being closed."

PEOPLE just can't stop talking about Donald Trump. A reader asks us: "Do you think that on his inauguration day, the secret service had to shoot down hundreds of armed time travellers from the future?"

PLANS by Glasgow City Council for a £9 million facelift of Byres Road reminds us of one our our favourite stories about the road when an open-topped campaign bus was being driven down the thoroughfare campaigning for the late, great Janey Buchan to be elected for Labour. The police flagged the bus down and told the driver that, if the wee guy on the top deck with the microphone didn't stop swearing, then the bus would be put off the road.

It seems his microphone-distorted chant of "Vote Buchan, Labour" had been misheard.

THE Article 50 ruling was of course big news yesterday. The *Edinburgh Evening News* reported: "*Outlander* star Sam Heughan has voiced his dismay at the Scottish Parliament being denied a vote on Article 50."

This proved too much for Tory MSP Murdo Fraser who took to social media to ask: "Does anyone know what view Jedward take on the Supreme Court judgment? Vital that we are told."

READERS tell us they were drawn, like watching a car crash, to the coverage of Donald Trump's inauguration. There was even criticism of his stilted shuffling when he ushered wife Melania on to the floor at his Inauguration Ball. As Jack Lattimore put it: "You'd think Trump has had enough weddings to learn how to waltz."

And our favourite placard on the huge protest march the following day in Washington - "Melania, Blink Twice If You Need Help".

WE are obsessing about Donald Trump's New York headquarters. Says Malcolm McCalister: "When in New York a while back I was enjoying the sights of the city from an open-top bus. When we passed Trump Tower, the guide commented that Mr

Trump was not in that day as he was attending the birth of his next wife."

SOME folk were getting agitated about SNP MP Hannah Bardell wearing a football top in the House of Commons.

Former Falkirk MP Dennis Canavan recalls: "At last a sartorial revolution at Westminster with Speaker Bercow ruling that MPs don't need to wear a tie and Hannah Bardell sporting a Scotland jersey. Changed days since the 1980s when a Tory MP complained that I was not wearing a tie.

"Speaker Thomas pompously responded that any tieless MP would fail to catch his eye, which is a euphemism for not getting called to speak. I politely asked if that would also apply to the prime minister. As this was during the Thatcher regime, Speaker Thomas suddenly realised the absurdity of his ruling and moved on to next business."

OH, and on the subject of politics, John Neil cheekily asks: "A fellow on the radio this morning was saying the Tories were like 'rats fighting in a sack'. Why do rats always get such a bad press?"

WORRYING thought from Bruce Skivington who claims: "You do realise Donald Trump, as a property owner in Scotland and with Scottish citizenship through his mother, could vote here and stand for election. He could end up as First Minister."

SOME terrible weather on election day. A reader heard a fellow customer in a Glasgow pub berating his mate for not bothering to vote. His pal came back with: "No' even Gene Kelly would go out in that rain!"

Talking of the election, we liked Simon Blackwell who commented: "At the polling station. Bodes well for Labour - loads of young people here. Or I might possibly be at the wrong primary school."

WELL, that's the election nearly over, thank goodness. Tory candidate Nadine Dorries used social media to declare, and I am quoting exactly: "Some Conservative posters have been daubed with swass stickers."

Inevitably someone asked: "Are these like the football stickers you can buy in the newsagents?"

IAIN McGill, the Tory hopeful in Edinburgh North & Leith, had a flashback to his previous role as a postie the other day.

Canvassing in Pilrig he came to a door with a sign saying "If out, please leave packages with neighbour".

At the next house, there was another sign. "Please do not leave packages for neighbours here," it said firmly.

MORE on the council elections as we hear that old chum Paul Drury is standing as an independent candidate in Giffnock and Thornliebank to stop a housing development. Paul tells us: "Proofreading my newsletter, I noticed a mistake in the date of the election. I tried to be polite, and gently suggested to the printer, 'I think we'll change the date of the election to May 4.' "He replied, 'Wow. No' even in yet and you can change the Polling Day. Impressive'."

GLASGOW Lord Provost Sadie Docherty is giving up her post come the council elections next month. During her five years in office she has been a guest at hundreds of events but we always liked the tale of her attending a fundraising sporting dinner for the Beatson at Glasgow's Hilton Hotel, wearing her chain of office, where former boxing champ Frank Bruno referred to her as "the madam here with the bling".

AFTER talk of Spain and Britain going to war over Gibraltar, a Scottish exile in England says he wants to come home after a colleague sent him the following gag: "Gibraltar declared war on Spain and the Spanish President replied, 'don't you know that we have 75,000 troops?'. The Chief Minister of Gibraltar discussed this with his ministers and then replied to Spain that the war was off. When asked why he replied, 'We haven't enough room for so many POWs.'"

THE meeting this week of Donald Trump and the old diplomat Henry Kissinger reminds a reader of the Kissinger quote: "Ninety per cent of politicians give the other 10 per cent a bad reputation."

HOW Tory is new East Renfrewshire MP Paul Masterton? Very, judging by his past life on Twitter. In 2015, he asked the makers of the "Glasgow as F***" T-shirt line: "I don't suppose you have a 'Tory as F***' range? I'm thinking maybe in a nice royal blue?" He was disappointed. "We prefer to see products people want to buy," came the shirty reply.

LABOUR'S only Scottish MP Ian Murray has been left embarrassed after sending a leaflet out to voters claiming to list "some of my achievements" on the reverse of the letter. The other side was blank.

He blamed a printing error.

TRUMP continues his craziness in America. James Martin comments: "Fitting that Trump's links with Russia seem to involve a little lie, inside a slightly bigger lie, in another larger lie..."

5

School's Out

The best days of our lives some folk say. Other disagree. But whatever your view, *Herald* readers have vivid memories of their time at school and share their funniest recollections with us.

A GLASGOW teacher, watching the Primary 7 go away on a week's residential trip, recalls teaching in a Bridgeton school in the seventies when she asked a young lad what he liked best about being away on a week-long school trip.

"Miss, it was great," he replied. "The best thing was I got a bed to masel - naebody kicked me a' week."

AN Ayrshire reader says that there are things we do at school that we never do again in our lives. He gives as examples:

* Putting your hand up to ask to go to the toilet.

* Holding buttercups up to your chin to see if you like butter.

* Putting your chair on your desk at the end of a day's work.

* Running screaming to the window when you see a dog outside.

SCHOOL'S almost finished for the year and it cannot come quick enough for a Glasgow primary teacher who tells us: "Among the arithmetic question I set my class was, 'It is 5.45pm and you are meeting someone at 6.15pm, how long do you have to wait?' One of the pupils wrote, 'Not long'."

OUR recent school stories remind Amy Kinnaird: "Years ago there were three boys called John in the primary class I taught.

"One afternoon, as I brought the lines in after lunch-time, I noticed one John was missing. I asked his pal, another John, where he was and was told the toilet.

"After the class settled I realised that he was still not in the room and I sent his pal to see what was wrong.

"After a few minutes the classroom door was dramatically thrown open, nearly hitting the wall, and John announced to myself and the whole class, 'He's OK, Mrs Kinnaird. He's just doing a jobbie. I heard a plop'. The class erupted."

TEACHERS are now counting down the days to the summer holidays. One Glasgow teacher tells us she once had a lad who told her with a big grin that his dog had eaten his homework. When she said she didn't believe him, he added: "He did - but I had to smear it with peanut butter first."

SOMEHOW we stumbled into tales of primary school toilets, and Ian Forrest reminds us: "When my stepfather was teaching a new P1 intake at Edzell Primary, one wee lad fae up the glens was excused to go to the toilet. Several minutes later he reappeared and asked in a loud voice, 'Wha aboot here wipes erses?'"

"Poor fastidious John, a bachelor until 50, had to do the honours."

CHILDREN at school, continued. Says retired teacher Moira Campbell: "One day a colleague put in the school notices that she had stick insects and if anyone wanted one they had to bring a jar and a bit of privet hedge. This confused my second years. I overheard one ask, 'Is that a hedge round a garden and not a park?' His pal replied, 'I thought it was toilet in the garden'. I told the teacher to just say hedge next time."

SCHOOL camps continued. Says Ada McDonald in Cambuslang: "Dumbarton Education Authority in the mid-1950s had a residential school near Drymen for summer camps where I offered my services. After a fairly active day outdoors, I got them settled down and I happily headed for an early night. I was interrupted by a knock on the door accompanied by much stifled giggling. 'We couldnae sleep miss'. I sent them back to their room still giggling and could clearly hear: 'See, Ah tell't ye she wouldnae use curlers'."

GLASGOW Academy's new science block has been awarded the Best Building in Scotland award for this year.

Among the former pupils of the West End private school is Radio Scotland and former rugby star John Beattie, who once explained that, although he went to a private school, his family was by no means well off.

He added: "I remember reading a passage at school about some guy taking the Rolls out.

"Everyone else in the class knew it referred to a car. I thought it was bread."

EUNAN Coll in Coatbridge tells us: "The story is told of John O'Leary, an Irish Ryder Cup golfer of the seventies, who sported big hair at the time, being seated at a hairdresser's in Dublin having a trim. 'You attended Blackrock College didn't you?' asked the barber. 'How do you know that?' replied John. 'I've just come across your school cap,' said the hairdresser.

NEIL in Hull tells us: "My son's friend Ian thought his teacher liked his story because she wrote 'Magic ian!' in the margin. Sadly, she was correcting his spelling of magician."

WE ended our school toilet stories but Grant Young manages to combine school toilets with our other thread, getting the belt, by telling us: "When I attended Ayr Academy, the toilets were a haunt of smokers, and offered a fair chance of escape from PE Principal Jock McLure's occasional raids, as when he charged in one end, the smokers would disappear out the opposite end.

"One day, I was, as a committed non-smoker, standing doing what the toilets were designed for doing when the smokers scarpered when Jock stormed in. I was ordered to his office where I duly received six of the best from his Lochgelly. He said that as the only person there I must have warned the smokers."

IT seems like a long time to parents, but most schools finally got back this week after the Christmas and New Year holiday. A West End reader tells us he heard a young mother explain: "I like these 20 mile-an-hour speed limits around the school. It makes texting so much easier."

IT was hard not to sympathise yesterday with the Scottish pupils - and their parents, of course - who anxiously awaited the SQA exam certificates. Naturally, many of them took to Twitter to express their apprehension at the endless wait, an attitude summed up by one mother who tweeted: "Omg, where the hell is the bloody postie? Don't they know I have a daughter that's freakin out?"

Not everyone else was entirely sympathetic, though - witness the person who wrote: "If I was a postman today I'd drive everywhere at 10mph just to add to the tension."

"Don't worry about your exam results young ones", someone else counselled. "I passed all of mine and I'm still miserable and hate my job."

GETTING old continued. Says a Newton Mearns reader: "Remember when teachers didn't like you using a calculator in class as they told you, 'You won't always have a calculator with you'. They got that wrong, didn't they?"

MORE on what you did at school, but never since. Says Derek McKay: "I haven't made a hat out of a poly bag to get home in the rain since leaving school. If the 5p levy was about in the 80s, half of Coatbridge would have been riddled with pleurisy."

VERBAL misunderstandings continued. Says Carol Johnston in Ayr: "Growing up in dear old Cumnock, I was friendly with a local doctor's daughter.

"Over dinner, her family were discussing a music exam we had just sat.

"Her mother announced, 'I hear Carol got merit'. Their little boy piped up, 'Merrit mummy? Is she not too young?' "He was whisked off to private school in Edinburgh shortly afterwards."

OUR school caps stories stumbled into the dark world of corporal punishment and our old pal Gerry Burke tells us that his old school St Aloysius carried on with the belt after it had been abandoned in state schools. A group of pupils, amongst them future lawyers and journalists, gathered in Partick station waiting room to compose a highly indignant and lengthy letter to *The Herald* to decry the practice.

By the time they were finished they reckoned it was too late to go to school and dogged off to the nearby Rosevale Cinema.

Someone clyped to the school - and yes they were all given the belt the next day.

GROWING old, continued. Says Janet Guthrie: "When I was teaching quite a few years ago I recall feeling ancient when a girl in my primary class excitedly told me she was going to Stepps on Saturday. 'That's nice, are you visiting your gran?' I asked. The puzzled look on her face said it all. 'Steps is a pop group, Miss!'"

BEFORE we put our tawse stories back in the drawer, Sandra Scott tells us: "I was a teacher at Whitehill Secondary on the last day of term before the belt would be banned by law. That afternoon a teacher came over the Tannoy to say if anyone wanted to be belted on this historic day they were to report to the headteacher's office.

"A queue formed down the stairs and the volunteers were belted 'live on air' over the Tannoy."

WE asked what you did at school, but never since, and George Crawford reminds us: "Re-folding Spangles and Opal Fruits wrappers to trick people into thinking that they still contained sweets."

WE mentioned school toilets, and Tom Bradshaw cheers us up with: "I was headteacher at St Thomas Aquinas Secondary in Glasgow and until 2003 the building was in a poor state of repair.

"It was best summed up by a young lad who said to me one morning, 'Sir, I wouldn't go into the boys toilet, it's like the Black Hole of Kentucky'.

"I took his word for it."

WHAT you did at school but never since: Moira Campbell says: "We used to have a competition in the dining hall to see which table could get a spoon to stand up the longest in what passed for custard," and Jack Petrie in East Kilbride recalls: "Taking a lump of chewing gum out of my mouth, pulling it apart, and giving a piece to my pal."

JAMIE Rae says: "All chanting good morning to the boss in unison before starting a day's work," and David Donaldson recalls: "Back then I could hit a lug-hole at 10 paces using only a Bic pen casing and some pearl barley."

ENTERTAINER Andy Cameron says: "There are three things I don't miss. Rubbing Calamine lotion on the scurvy mark on my legs left by my wellies. Sitting raging in the 'sound effects' section in Mr Mooney's music class.

"Last, but not least, being conned into a 'square go' at four o'clock against the best fighter in the school - I beat her by the way."

ALISON Ireland in Kirn was one of a number of ladies who told us: "Running about in public with my blouse tucked in my navy blue knickers."

FANS are getting excited about the impending seventh series of the bloodthirsty fantasy series *Game of Thrones*. It reminds us of the Belgian teacher a few years back who was trying to quieten an unruly class. He eventually told them: "I know you are fans of *Game of Thrones*. Just to say I've read all the books, and if you don't shut up I'll write on the board the name of the next person who dies in it."

The class went silent.

6

Taking the Oath

Not everyone's dealings with courts and the police are a laughing matter, but when they do bring a smile then we were happy to retell them in *The Herald.*

IT'S great the way the police are using social media to contact people. The other day Yorkshire Police in Kirklees posted a picture of a wedding couple and asked: "Do you recognise this couple? A wedding album featuring them was found dumped in a bin in Holmforth and we'd like to give it back."

Only an hour later the police then added: "Mystery solved. Looks like the album was handed into us in good faith, but the owner doesn't want it back."

TALKING of the excitable news stories about folk dressing up as clowns to scare people, even Police Scotland has warned folk could get into trouble for doing so.

Inevitably, a Newton Mearns father could not stop himself from telling his 17-year-old daughter getting ready for a night out: "I'd go easy on that make-up if I were you. Wouldn't want someone reporting you to the police over this clown craze."

I WAS reminiscing with an old pal about the days when your car had a separate radio screwed into the car and the radio was often stolen by thieves. He told me of a mate who had to park his car in a dodgy part of the city overnight, and who left a note on the dashboard stating "Radio broken."

He returned the following day to find the radio had been nicked, with someone scrawling on the note "We'll fix it".

WE can just imagine. As Levenmouth Police announced yesterday on social media: "Theft of non-alcoholic lager from

Leven Toon Centre. We're looking for one disappointed thief."

A RETIRED police officer swears to us that a woman once phoned the police office to report her cat was missing. The officer who took the call tried to tell her they could nothing at all about a missing cat, but she insisted: "But he's very intelligent. Almost human. He can almost speak to me."

"Well you'd better hang up," the officer told her, "Just in case he's trying to call you right now."

READER John Neil wonders if Scottish court cases have become a lot more serious than they used to be. He only asks as he came across an old *Evening Times* from the 1960s with a report from Hamilton Sheriff Court which began: "A man who had been thrown out of a Lanarkshire pub during a late-night party sat on the pavement outside, unfastened his artificial legs - and threw them through the pub windows."

WE like *Mrs Brown's Boys* creator Brendan O'Carroll's colourful description of his time in Borstal after being caught shoplifting. He told the *Radio Times*: "I was no fool. On my first day there, I was in the canteen and the older boys said, 'So what are ya in for?' and I said, 'I killed me Da'. And they said, 'What?' And I said, 'I killed me Da. I stuck a pen through his eye'. And nobody came near me."

AFTER the news that the penalty for using your mobile phone while driving has increased, Bruce Skivington tells us: "I hear that police stopped a car and said it was an offence to use your phone while driving and the occupant readily agreed.

"It was when the officer said he was going to be charged that the occupant said, 'Let me stop you. You do realise this is a Polish registered vehicle and is left-hand drive?'"

POLICE Scotland took to social media to ask the public to vote on the name for their new police horse - a grey draught horse from Ireland. As their horses have Scottish place names, the four names to choose from were Melrose, Clarkston, Glencoe and Tiree - Glencoe won. But we liked the thinking process of one member of the public, Martin Gray, who replied to Police Scotland: "Not Melrose, because they always beat us at Sevens. Not Glencoe because of the Campbells. And not Clarkston because I canna stand the bloke and all that *Top Gear* rubbish. So it's got to be Tiree."

ROSS Harper, the Glasgow lawyer, has written his memoir, *Beyond Reasonable Doubt*, which is published next week. In it, he recalls the recidivist Barney Noone who previously made the Diary when Sheriff Irvine Smith sentenced him with the ditty: "Thirty days hath November, April, June and Barney Noone". Anyway, Ross says that Barney came to court after going into a hairdresser's for a shave and haircut, and afterwards telling the barber he had to nip out to his car for his cash.

Instead he went into a shoe-shop, chose a pair, and again used the excuse of going to his car for money. He then hailed a taxi, took it to near his house, and said he had to go inside for his money, but left his new shoes in their box as security. When he did not return the taxi driver opened the shoebox to find Barney's decrepit old shoes.

WE also liked Ross's recollection that his former boss Jimmy Martin, a bit of a rough diamond, once told the story of being a youthful car-park attendant at a racecourse. Wrote Ross: "When people parked, he would give them a tip. He would pick a race in which there were six or more runners, and he would sidle up and whisper the name of the horse and say, 'Back it. It's going to win'. He gave the next car owner another horse until he had tipped them all to win, making sure he remembered which car he had tipped so he could identify the winner when he came to his car."

WE are reminded by Ross of the late great advocate Lionel Daiches who had a liquid lunch before consulting with one of Ross's clients at Barlinnie before a High Court trial. After telling the client how the trial would proceed he asked if he had any questions. "No questions, Mr Daiches," said the client, "but just breathe on me once more."

THE news story that two prisoners at Pentonville Prison in London escaped after leaving life-size mannequins in their beds puzzles a reader who phones to ask: "Surely it's much more difficult to smuggle two life-size mannequins into a prison than actually escape?"

OUR mention of Campbell's soup reminds Bill Dalgleish in Sanquhar: "In my early days in the furniture trade I visited a customer and noticed all his garden equipment was out on the lawn. My casual remark of 'clearing out?' brought the response, 'No, helping the polis'.

"A goods train had derailed and thrown thousands of tins of Campbell's soup over the main road, and to get it cleared quickly, locals had been invited to help themselves to a 'few' cans. He opened the door of his hut and showed me a six foot by four foot solid block of soup. Public-spirited citizens like that just aren't around nowadays."

STILL trying to rein in our police horse stories as Alastair Donald in Langholm tells us: "My brother David was once astride his trusty polis horse at Ibrox, chivvying the turnstile queue into a semblance of order when he sensed his mare beneath him settle down for a pee.

"Immediately as said emission hit the tarmac, a Rangers fan opined, 'Awe typical - nae cups in the machine'."

TALKING of police horses, Manchester Police reported on social media: "Sun's out, and we've had a few calls to alcohol issues already. Latest is a man who has defecated in a pub beer garden."

A chap named Iain Macdonald replied: "Surely that's not illegal. Police horses do it all the time in the street."

But the police replied: "If you see a drunk police horse do one in a beer garden, let us know."

BEFORE we close the stable door on police horse stories, Gerry MacKenzie reminds us of the classic: "I was policing a match at Hampden when one inebriated chap, wolfing on a pudding supper, got fed up being dunted into line and hurled the black pudding at the offending police horse. The pudding smacked the mounted officer square on the shiny buttons, just as the culprit flung away the brown paper wrapper.

"He cantered over, stretched down and grabbed the guy by the collar, who screamed, 'It wisnae me'. 'Show's yer teeth' demanded the cop. The ned offered up a hideous smile and the mountie roared 'Yer teeth are a' puddin.' He got the pokey."

ALL right, we give in. Great swathes of readers have asked why we have not recounted the classic police horse in Glasgow story amongst our horse yarns. So for the sake of nostalgia, it is of course the female mounted police officer at Hampden holding back the crowds as one fan shouts up to her: "Your horse is sweatin'!" All together now: "So would you be if you'd been between ma legs all mornin'" she shouted back.

OUR court stories remind George Tomlinson of a lawyer pal, defending a Glasgow rascal accused of armed robbery, who told him his client went into the building society and told staff to lie on the floor before adding: "And lie on your bellies - this is not the office party."

OUR story about the new section of the M8 at Newhouse

reminds Matt Vallance: "Back in 1960, around the time of the Rome Olympics, my gaffer was done for speeding on that stretch of what was then the A8. This was before the police used radar, so he was timed by two polis over a measured section, and, when stopped, he was told how fast his time for the measured section had been.

"Being a Glaswegian, he replied, 'Great, what colour of medal do I get?'"

MONKLANDS Police tweeted details of the theft of £600 of Boots cosmetics. "We are looking", it declared with a straight face, "for a 40 y/o man who looks 20, glowing skin, long eyelashes, raised eyebrows & pronounced lips".

A READER much enjoyed *The Bridgeton Press*, a compilation of local stories available in Bridgeton Library.

It includes the newspaper cutting from 1953 of the Bridgeton woman appearing in court, accused of obtaining free drinks in public houses by pretending she was ill.

She started in a pub in Heron Street, where she said she was unwell and in need of a stimulant, and induced the charge-hand to give her a brandy. The suspicious barman followed her to two further bars where she did the same trick before he called the police. Nice try.

WE'VE not had a tale from the courts for a while and George Tomlinson was reminiscing with a chum about a mutual friend, now departed, who was a lawyer in Glasgow, who also liked a wee refreshment. On one occasion at Glasgow Sheriff Court he was not doing so well in his arguments when the Sheriff inquired if he had been drinking. "Just a little coq au vin for lunch, your honour,' he replied.

GROWING old continued. An inspector with the city centre office of Greater Manchester Police announced on social media yesterday: "Felt old this morning coming in for earlies, as much younger people still turning out of several clubs in city centre." Incidentally it was the same police office which recently told the story: "Man refused entry to club argues with door staff, passing phone to randomer in queue to record the altercation. Randomer runs off with phone."

WE mentioned court stories and reader John Hart swears to us that a witness in a bank robbery claimed she could identify an accused as it had been a hot day and they had removed their masks at one stage. One of the accused was heard muttering: "That's a lie. Never took them off."

AFTER our story about Police Scotland always naming their horses after Scottish place names, a reader swears blind that when the old Strathclyde force acquired a white horse, it was named Larkhall.

And sports writer Matt Vallance recalls: "Years ago I turned up early at Kilmarnock's Rugby Park, to find one of the mounties doing dressage moves with his horse in the car park. When I asked why, I was told, 'He's a bit frisky today, so, if I don't work him to calm him down, he'll probably kick a few fans, just for the hell of it'."

WE hold our hands up to running bank robbery stories, and Gerry McElroy in Cumbernauld says: "I heard about a robbery in a Shettleston shop where an arrest was made. The shopkeeper was taken to the police station to identify the suspect, but he said he couldn't as he had put a paper bag over his head. Whereupon a constable was sent to the Co-op next door, returned with a paper bag, put it on the accused's head and the shopkeeper immediately said: 'Yes, that's him'."

BROADCAST news can sometimes make our reader smile. Says Ian Barnett: "*STV News* announced that police are going to do more spot checks. Chic Murray's line springs to mind as Chic once put it, 'I was stopped by the police last night - they said it was a spot check. I admitted to two pimples and a boil'."

THE *Herald*'s archive picture of the busy fruitmarket in Albion Street reminds Gilbert McKay of cycling through the market on his way to his teaching job in Townhead. He was stopped one morning by a police officer, a member of the police pipe band, who said: "We need more youngsters in the force, and the band's short of pipers." I could be wrong, but I think the recruitment process is a bit more complicated these days.

THE 200th anniversary this year of the birth of renowned Glasgow architect Alexander "Greek" Thomson reminds us of the Scottish tabloid newspaper reporting on the death of Glasgow gangster Arthur Thompson. The sub-editor working on the story, presumably a fan of Damon Runyon, thought he recalled the deceased thug's nickname and referred to him through the story as Arthur "The Greek" Thompson.

CRAIG Whyte's brief, Donald Findlay, is reaping much praise for his incisive questioning during the fraud case. We recall attending a charity dinner at Ibrox where Donald told the classic tale of one of his clients, not a friend of the police, being questioned by detectives, who asked him where he had been between seven and eleven.

"Primary school," he replied.

7

A Four-Legged Friend

It has become the standard for people to send pictures of animals around the internet to cheer everyone up. *Herald* readers go one better by sending us their favourite pet and animal stories.

A HYNDLAND reader tries to convince us he was in a bookshop when a customer came in and asked if they had any books on turtles. The assistant asked: "Hard back?" the customer replied: "Yes, with little heads."

A READER phones to tell us: "Saw some ducks practising their teenage girls' faces at the pond today."

OUR story about the soup tins spilled over a road reminds Ian Petrie in Newton Stewart: "Many years ago a lorry loaded with Master McGrath dog food came off the A75 and landed in a field, just along from the factory where I worked. The load was lying everywhere. We were sent down to help clear up.

Naturally, many 'damaged' tins were being taken for dogs at home.

"One guy was filling the boot of his car and was asked if he had a dog. 'No' he said 'but ma mither takes in lodgers'.

"We hoped he was joking."

TODAY'S piece of whimsy comes from a reader who says: "Apparently, if you're being chased by a bear you should play dead. Sounds suspiciously like something a bear would say."

A READER sees the *Sky News* heading "Animal death zoo loses its license" and he thinks to himself: "Probably didn't help, having a name like that."

THE *Herald*'s archive picture of a Kelvin Hall circus elephant reminds retired journalist Graham Scott: "The late Rodney

Duncan of the *Evening Times* was sent to cover 'a day in the life of the circus', in which he lay on his back while an elephant stepped over him.

"Unfortunately, said elephant dropped what in the photo looked like a brick on Rod and his suit on the way over.

"After initial amusement, colleagues forgot about it until a week later when, in Ross's Bar, a certain smell made clear to anyone near him that Rodney had not bothered to have the suit cleaned."

AS MPs criticise the government for halting a study into the menace of seagulls, we are reminded of the cheeky chap in Edinburgh who, after drink had been taken, found a dead seagull on the road. He picked it up, went into his local takeaway, slammed it on the counter and said: "That's the last one I supply till you've paid for the rest."

There was then a sudden exit by everyone waiting for food.

OUR story about not being keen on housework reminds Cindy Paterson: "Our first dog, Katy, used to jump up at the window to see who was coming to visit whenever I got the Hoover out."

A READER out walking in Rouken Glen Park yesterday to clear his head heard a woman shouting ineffectually on her dog to come back. She told him as he tried to help: "He also ignores me when I whistle. I'm now trying to perfect imitating the sound of the fridge door opening, which is bound to work."

OUR stories of seagulls remind Norrie Christie: "Music hall singer Mal Hollander was driving me from Aberdeen to Glasgow in the late sixties, and cars going in the opposite direction were flashing their lights and drivers were waving at Mal. When I drew his attention to this he brushed it aside by saying, 'I'm pretty well known up here - people recognise me'.

"However further south, driving slowly through Perth, I noticed the car's reflection in a shop window and spread-eagled across Mal's roof-rack was a badly stunned seagull."

TODAY's piece of whimsy comes from Alan Maguire who says: "I'm watching two crows fight over a toothbrush.

"Crows don't even have teeth. It's just capitalism making them want things they don't need."

AN Edinburgh reader swears to us he was in his local coffee shop where a young woman rushed in to join her pals and told them: "Sorry

I'm late. I tripped over my cat and had to stroke him for 20 minutes."

A SOUTHSIDE reader tells us it was surely unfair of someone who had written on a poster an anxious animal owner had stuck to a lamppost seeking help in finding missing cat, "Cats know where they live. Your cat didn't like you".

TODAY'S piece of daftness comes from a Renfrewshire reader who emails: "When I was young my parents used to make me walk the plank. We couldn't afford a dog."

GOOD news! The Lobey Dosser statue, paid for by *Herald* readers to mark the genius of Dosser creator Bud Neill, has been returned to its plinth in Woodlands Road after some much-needed repairs by Glasgow Council. I remember my old colleague Jack Webster once recounting that Bud Neill lived beside a cemetery - so called his house Dim View. At that time he worked from a converted post office outside Dunfermline where he was occasionally bothered by folk peering in. So he put up a blind in the window, and on a whim put a poster on the outside of the blind on which he had written "Budgies repaired Saturdays".

THE news story about the fox-hunting trial in the Borders brings forth the comment from a Glasgow reader: "I don't know why hunting is called a sport. Is it really a sport when one team doesn't know the match has started?"

WE mentioned inspired cartoonist Bud Neill, and Ian Millar recalls: "My father once worked for Cambuslang butcher Adam Chapman, who bred the occasional litter of Great Danes and sold a puppy to Bud Neill. Not having heard anything about the pup for some time, Mr Chapman rang up for a progress report. 'Great Dane?', said Mr Neill. 'Da'in great!'"

WE mentioned cartoonist Bud Neill, whose Lobey Dosser statue has been repaired, having a Great Dane. A reader tells us: "As a child, my route to my primary school took me past his house. Aged eight, I was very nervous of 'normal' dogs but this Great Dane was a step too far. It would emerge from its gate, put its paws on my shoulders and look me in the eye. My mother got frequent phone calls from acquaintances asking her to come and rescue me."

8

Your Other Half

Keeping a relationship fresh and alive, or even embarking on one, has its pitfalls. *Herald* readers share their thoughts on falling in love and the problems it brings.

A GLASGOW reader tells us he heard a new take on the marriage split of showbiz couple Brad Pitt and Angelina Jolie when he heard it being discussed by a group of woman in his Partick local at the weekend.

One of the women opined: "I knew they weren't in it for the long haul when neither of them let themselves go."

A READER hears a young man out for a pint in Glasgow tell his pals: "I bought my girlfriend a fridge for her birthday. Not a great gift I know, but you should have seen her face light up when she opened it."

THE most crushing comment we are sent this week is from a reader who passed on a message from a young man who told his pals: "I was the only one in a lift when an attractive girl came in, talking on her phone. She told her friend, 'I have to go, there's a cute guy here.' Before I could even react, she turned to me and said, 'Sorry for lying, I really wanted to get off the phone with her."

OUR gag about opticians yesterday reminds a reader: "I was at the wedding of an optician where the minister said to his future wife, 'Do you, Karen, take David the optician to be your lawfully wedded husband, for better or worse? Better ... or worse? Better... or worse?"

IT seems Scotsmen may have a lot in common with their counterparts in Finland. A reader sends us a survey on dating etiquette around the world which states public displays of affection in Finland are uncommon. It adds: "There is a Finnish joke that men there say 'I love you' twice - on their wedding day and on their deathbed."

WE were chatting to a reader who tells us: "I was worried about my husband finding his birthday present before his big day, but then I suddenly knew what to do. I put it in a kitchen cupboard with just one item in front of it - he wouldn't find it in a million years."

WE'VE not had any wedding speech stories for a while so thank you to the Stirling reader who tells us the best man recently ended his speech by announcing: "As you might know, me and my wonderful girlfriend have been together for five years. I've had a few drinks but I hope you'll indulge me if I ask her a very special question." He then rummaged in his pocket, and as tension in the room rose, he finally fished out his car keys and said: "I'm a bit drunk love. Could you drive home?"

WE mentioned wedding speeches, and Russell Smith in Kilbirnie comments: "During his remarks at a wedding reception which I attended, the minister informed us that at a previous wedding the groom had given his bride a nightie and his bride had given him a Bible. He added that if he had lifted the Bible as often as he had lifted the nightie he could have been the Moderator of the General Assembly of the Church of Scotland."

A READER hears a young chap on the train into Glasgow tell his pals: "I always stand in the middle when the girlfriend wants a group photo. It's going to make it difficult for her to crop me out if we ever split up."

A READER in a Glasgow pub at the weekend heard a young toper tell his pals: "My wife was at a girlie night out at the Corinthian last week and said some guy bought her drinks all night, and was I jealous. I told her, 'Absolutely. I wish someone would buy me drinks all night'."

TRICKY stuff the dating business. A reader in a Glasgow pub hears a young chap tell his pals: "I tried one of those dating sites and came across a good-looking woman from the West End. Then I read under 'What she was looking for in a man'. She had written, 'Someone who will hold my cats while I take pictures of them wearing sunglasses'. Decided to pass."

A WEST End reader swears to us he was in a Byres Road pub when a young woman looking at her phone told her pals: "My boyfriend just texted 'We need to talk'. Do you think he's going to propose?"

WE were in a city centre pub where some married chaps were discussing changes in their relationships. Eventually one piped up: "Before I got married, my future wife would text me saying, 'I'm not wearing any underwear.' Now she'll text me saying, 'I'm not wearing any underwear - because you didn't put the laundry in the dryer like I asked you 100 times'."

A BEARSDEN reader emails us with the following advice: "It really is important your wife knows you're patting the dog when she hears you say, 'you're getting a bit on the chunky side these days'."

MARRIED life was being discussed in a Glasgow pub the other night where one toper opined: "About three-quarters of being married is just shouting, 'What?' from another room."

A READER hears a woman in the West End tell her pals: "I just want a man who'll drag me to the bedroom, throw me on the bed and do the dishes while I take a nap. Is that too much to ask for?"

A MILNGAVIE reader swears to us he saw a friend leaving the local florist's shop with a plant. When he asked him who it was for he replied: "The wife. We had a bit of an argument - but not a huge dozen red roses type of argument."

A PARTICK reader passes on the words of wisdom of a regular in his local pub who declared at the weekend: "No one is more productive than someone who's been lying on the couch for two hours and suddenly realises his wife will be home in five minutes."

SOMEHOW we stumbled into stories about artificial limbs, and David Donaldson swears to us: "The husband of a tea lady we employed in the early eighties had an artificial leg and one of her marital sanctions was to put his leg on top of the wardrobe. Once, when he came home much the worse for drink, she was was so angry she whipped it off him and threw it out of the landing window into the back green three floors below."

DAFT gag from a chap in a Glasgow pub at the weekend who told his pals: "Went back to my new girlfriend's flat and asked her what the scary photo on her hall table was. 'That's my X-Ray,' she said. So I told her, 'I don't know what's worse - the fact you dated a skeleton or that its name was Ray."

RELATIONSHIP advice from a reader who says: "When out for a meal with the wife, always order the same dish as she does. That way you don't lose half your meal when she says, 'Can I taste a bit of yours?'"

A SIGN of the times says a Hyndland reader who heard a woman meet her pal in a Byres Road coffee shop and tell her that she was looking good. "Thanks," replied her pal, "I think it's the divorce."

A GLASGOW reader in his local heard the latest chapter in the constant attempt by the two sexes to understand each other. One of the locals told him: "I told the wife she looked very pretty today. So apparently what I really said was, 'You look ugly every day except for today'."

A READER heard some chaps in a Glasgow pub discussing

horoscopes and what a load of baloney they were, although one toper piped up: "I always read my wife's horoscope to see what kind of day I'm going to have."

A READER emails: "My girlfriend says I'm hopeless at fixing appliances. Well, she's in for a shock."

A COLLEAGUE was heading like an arrow towards me so I knew he wanted to tell me a story. "The missus accused me of being a crossdresser," he began.

I didn't react, but he carried on: "So I packed her things and left."

TODAY'S piece of whimsy comes from a reader who comments: "Before you get married, ask yourself this question, 'Is this the person I want to watch stare at their phone for the rest of my life?'"

A READER hears a loudmouth in a Glasgow bar declare: "The wife said to me, 'All our friends are having babies now.' "So I told her we should do something about that. I said we should go ahead and get new friends."

WE commend the sheer daftness of a reader who emails: "My wife left me because I'm too insecure.

"No wait, she's back. She had just gone to make a cup of tea."

WE hear a regular in a city centre pub moan to his pals: "The wife opened a new jar of beetroot the day without my help. I can't help but think that my days are numbered."

RELATIONSHIP worries continued. A female reader in Hyndland tells us: "Whenever I hear that two people I know are going out with each other, I immediately start worrying about whose side I'll be on when they break up."

TELEVISION show *Blind Date* is to be resurrected on Channel 5, it has been announced. It reminds us of the Glasgow woman who told her pals that her blind date the previous weekend had been a disaster.

"He picked me up in a vintage Rolls-Royce," she said. "What's wrong with that?" asked her mate.

"He was the original owner," she replied.

A HYNDLAND reader was impressed when the fridge/freezer suddenly packed in at the weekend and her husband announced: "I'll handle it'.

She didn't realise he possessed electrical skills but then ten minutes later she went into the kitchen and found he was simply sitting at the table eating a tub of ice cream.

TALKING of relationships, a reader heard a chap in his golf club explain: "I always regret making a good first impression, because there is no way I can keep that stuff going."

RELATIONSHIP difficulties continued. A Linlithgow reader hears a chap in his local declare: "The wife was screaming at me, 'I hope you're happy.' I don't think she meant it."

A GLASGOW reader swears to us he was in a West End pub at the weekend where a woman was bemoaning her inability to find a decent boyfriend. Eventually her pal told her: "Why don't you ask out the guy who delivered your curry last night? At least you know he's got a car, a job, and access to curry."

ANOTHER slice of the complex world of marital life as a reader in Glasgow hears a chap in his local declare: "I don't just put the seat down, I put the lid down as well. If I have to work to pee, then so does she."

COMEDIAN Phil Pagett is bringing his show *Bare Jokes* to the Edinburgh Fringe this year. We did like Phil's line: "My last girl-friend dumped me unexpectedly. I came home and she'd sold our house. I suppose I should've seen the signs."

A READER in a Glasgow pub at the weekend overheard a group of chums berating a pal for going out with a girl who was far too young for him.

"What do you base that on?" he argued with them.

"Based on the number of times the earth has orbited the sun since she was born," a pal shot back.

A READER tells us he heard a woman in a Southside coffee shop tell her pals, who all had jobs, that she was extremely busy even though she was a stay-at-home wife. She did add though: "My husband thinks that half my time is spent hiding his stuff in the house.

"He's daft - that only takes about a quarter of my time."

A READER in Partick goes all philosophical as he emails: "The human brain starts working the moment you're born, and never stops until your wife asks where you were last night."

A BISHOPBRIGGS reader emails: "Was driving behind a delivery van that had a sign on the side which said, 'Driver carries no money'. So I guessed he must be married."

RELATIONSHIPS continued. A West End reader swears to us he was in a Byres Road pub where some young women were berating a pal for getting off with a bit of a rogue at a party at the weekend. The girl replied: "I don't set out to make bad choices. But by the time I got to the party all the good choices were taken."

RELATIONSHIP advice - a Merchant City reader says he heard a toper in his local bar tell his pal who was about to get married: "If you want to know about marriage, it's a bit like a museum. You have to be quiet, and you can't really touch anything."

A GLASGOW reader heard a chap in his local musing to his pals: "It's funny isn't it. You meet someone's wee kid you've not seen for a while and everyone's all smiles when you say, 'Goodness, look how big you've got'.

"But say it to an ex-girlfriend and all hell breaks loose."

WE'VE mentioned the pitfalls of internet dating before, and a Shawlands reader tells us her pal put on her profile she was a Catholic. Some chap replied, asking: "How long have you been addicted to cats?"

A KNIGHTSWOOD reader says he was in a city-centre pub where a toper was telling his buddies: "The wife said she thought my best mate's girlfriend was a gold-digger and I should warn him about her.

"I told her I wasn't going to say anything, and when she asked me why not I told her, 'Well, he never warned me'."

WE are wary of relationship advice from a Glasgow pub, but we pass on from the chap in the city centre bar who told his pals: "If your girlfriend catches you staring at another woman, quickly tell her, 'I'm glad you don't dress like that'."

AH the philosophers of Glasgow pubs. A reader heard a toper opine the other night in his local: "Some people say marriage is like taking a bath - not so hot once you've been in it for a while".

9

I Know the Face

The Herald is not some celebrity magazine where we gush over folk we see on the telly. But our readers do bump into the stars and tell us about it.

FORMER *Taggart* stars Blythe Duff and John Michie are on stage at Glasgow's Tron Theatre next month in the thriller *Grain in the Blood*, a new production from playwright Rob Drummond. Blythe was in Australia earlier this year with *The James Plays*, and when asked about *Taggart* on a local radio station she told the lovely story that she was in *Taggart* for over 20 years and went up in rank from police constable to detective inspector. Her mum, she said, always asked her when she got a promotion if that meant more money.

VETERAN broadcaster Robbie Shepherd has been recording his last episode of country dance music show *Take the Floor* for

Radio Scotland. It somehow reminds us of Robbie writing in his book, *Dash o Doric*, that Harry Lauder left a concert on Deeside confused as to why his jokes had not gone down as well as in other venues. He cheered up, though, when he overheard a lady remark on the way out: "Fit a gran' comic. It took me aa' ma' time nae ti' laugh."

HAPPY birthday to American comic and actor Steve Martin who was 71 yesterday. He has been a frequent visitor to Scotland and once recalled: "The first time I came to Scotland I was 21. When I got off the train the streets were full of people laughing, drinking and puking. I thought this place was incredible ... and it's only Thursday.

"I assumed this was something that went on all the time. Then I learned these people were there for a rugby game between Scotland and Wales."

WE liked crusty old author Frederick Forsyth explaining that, when he finished writing his memoir *The Outsider*, he thought to himself: "Who have I insulted? Who might sue?" The 77-year-old was then relieved to conclude that "there were only two left alive".

MEANWHILE over at the Edinburgh Fringe, comedian Mark Steel, who likes to research the towns that he does his show in, was explaining that he once did a gig in Berwick, and discovered that it changed hands 14 times between Scotland and England. Added Mark: "When it was finally settled that it would be in

England, the mayor apparently said, 'Thank Christ for that. I couldn't stand another bloody Scottish winter'."

WE mentioned world-record-breaker cyclist Mark Beaumont appearing at the Edinburgh Book Festival, and a reader who was there tells us: "For cyclists in the audience, Mark gave away some of his long-distance cycling tips and tricks, which included stashing a spare $1,000 in his seat just in case. He then paused and added, 'Probably not a good trick of the trade to give away actually. Don't steal my bike'."

WE liked the response of presenter Dara O'Briain, who fronted the remake of *Robot Wars*, which was filmed in Glasgow. A fan asked him on social media: "Everyone says the arena is cold. How cold is it honestly?" Replied Dara: "A 'warehouse in Glasgow in January' cold."

WE pass on stand-up Jenny Eclair reflecting in the *Radio Times* on coping with growing old. Said Jenny: "I do know I've gone off - the last time I came through passport control and attempted the automatic biometric machine, it refused to believe I and my passport photo were the same woman - and yet my passport doesn't expire until 2018. 'It's the jowls,' said the nice security lady, 'and the wrinkles'."

ACTRESS Ruby Wax is doing a one-woman show at the Glasgow Citz next year. Ruby was a student at Glasgow Art College many years ago and she recalled recently: "I went to Glasgow before it was Starbucked to death - when it was just an ashtray with a couple of stop lights." Yes, happy days.

SINGING legend Bob Dylan is playing a gig in Glasgow next May. We recall a reader once telling us that he saw Bob in America where he actually told a joke. Bob introduced his drummer as "a guy who there wasn't nothing he wouldn't do for me, and there's nothing I wouldn't do for him - and we've been going through our whole life doing nothing for each other".

GROWING old continued. Glasgow-born *Dr Who* actor Peter Capaldi told the *Radio Times*: "I've got belts older than the actors I'm working with now."

SCOTS entertainer Johnny Beattie is 90 today. As the great man himself put it: "I'm nearly as old as my gags and that's saying something."

AH, drunks at the Edinburgh Fringe. Stand-up Patrick Monahan was heckled by five young men whom he dismissed as "trust fund kids" who were spoiling the night for everyone else, so the five stormed out, with one of them throwing a pint of beer at him.

We like Patrick's sangfroid as he merely told the audience who were booing the departing five: "Only a posh person would throw a full pint. An honest working-class person would have drunk it first and thrown the empty glass."

BROADCASTER Desmond Carrington has retired from his popular Radio 2 show *The Music Goes Round*. Reader Eric Hudson tells us: "He once had to play a recording of Rimsky-Korsakov's 'Flight Of The Bumble Bee', and was terrified he would stumble over the composer's name, so he went around all day saying 'Rimsky-Korsakov'. That night he confidently announced, 'Now here is a piece of music by Rimsky-Korsakov - The Bum Of The Flightle Bee'."

THE foul-mouthed comedian Roy Chubby Brown is appearing in Dunfermline and Inverness next month as part of his latest tour. It reminds us of his autobiography when Roy admitted he initially struggled in Scotland. He wrote: "The first night I played Penicuik working men's club, as rough a club as any. I lasted two minutes. The next night I was in Lesmahagow. Paid off after 10 minutes.

"On the Tuesday I played Rosyth naval yard. The wives loved me even more than the sailors did. Standing ovation. The following night I was paid off at Kilmarnock, at which point my agent suggested I came home. 'They don't know talent when they see it', he said."

CONGRATULATIONS to Rod Stewart on being knighted. We recall when the *New York Daily News* reported years ago that Rod, before a show at Madison Square Gardens, got "totally wasted" in a local bar.

It wrote: "He danced a number of jigs and sang folk songs,

including one remembered as 'You Can't Put Grandma on the Bus', though if a song by that name exists, it would be news to Google." We wondered if any Scot told them about the classic 'Ye Cannae Shove Yer Granny Aff A Bus'.

GOOD to see impassioned left-wing stand-up Mark Thomas appearing at The Tron in Glasgow. We recall when he did a May Day celebrations gig in Glasgow and handed out sticky labels - the type you see in bookshops - to audience members. The stickers read "Also Available in Charity Shops" and "Staff Recommendation: Keep the Receipt". He suggested folk surreptitiously put them on books by Tony Blair and Jeremy Clarkson when they were in a bookshop.

OH what larks. Glasgow humorist Brian Limond, of TV show *Limmy* fame, told his fans on social media after musing about the chaotic state of world politics: "I can feel a war coming on. A big one. Not a world war, but a Western one. Maybe 2022. Put all your money on it."

One of his fans, Jamie, took him at his word, contacted Sky Bet about Limmy's prediction and received the reply: "Hi Jamie, thanks for the request. Unfortunately, this is not something we would be able to price up."

COMEDY writer and former Python John Cleese is stirring things up it seems after taking umbrage at something written in a London magazine by a Scottish journalist. As Cleese fulminated:

"Why do we let half-educated tenement Scots run our English press? Because their craving for social status makes them obedient retainers."

We like the fact an American news site felt the need to add: "Tenement refers to high-density housing blocks in Edinburgh and Scotland, historically built to house the poor, leading to slum conditions in many parts."

Try telling that to the outraged folk in Glasgow's G12.

ACTUALLY, comedians having a go at Scots is not new - although on this occasion the comic actor was at least a fellow Scot. Says John Bannerman in Kilmaurs: "I was once in the posh Queen's Hotel in Leeds on business where I was joined in the lift by the late, great Scottish actor John Laurie of *Dad's Army* fame. I asked if I could have his autograph and he said, 'Certainly. What's your name? Have you got a piece of paper?' "I opened my packed case, and retrieved the sheets of hotel paper I had purloined. After signing, he jokingly remarked, 'Typical bliddy Scotsman!'"

TAKE That crooner Gary Barlow has announced he has a part in the next *Star Wars* film. A reader innocently asks: "Will he play Darth's other son, Taxi Vader?"

THAT great singer Emeli Sande is to perform at Edinburgh Castle in July. We well remember that before she was famous she did a gig at Oran Mor in Glasgow's West End which attracted some 500 punters, despite it being mid week.

Turned out that Emeli was performing under her real name of Adele and a few folk got confused abut who they were going to hear. It was a great gig anyway by all accounts.

BIRTHDAY greetings yesterday to singer Roger Whittaker, who was 81. Says Keith McClory: "I wonder if he ever did go back to Durham after all those years?"

BEACH Boys veteran Brian Wilson will be performing their great album *Pet Sounds* at Glasgow's Kelvingrove Park this summer. Says a Hyndland reader: "That reminds me of the old joke, 'The Beach Boys walk into a bar. 'Round?' 'Round'. 'Get a round'. 'I get a round'."

ACTOR Alex Norton is touring his one-man show, *There's Been A Life*, based on his autobiography.

We remember when Alex was at the city's Buchanan Bus Station filming a scene for *Taggart*, and standing around waiting, he watched the buses leaving before asking a fellow thespian: "Do you see that bus? Why would someone put 'Kill Malcolm X' on the front?" wondering whether it was some kind of political statement.

His colleague looked over before telling Alex: "It's Kilmacolm X, Alex - the bus is going to Kilmacolm Cross."

THE story about Ayr's Gaiety Theatre reminds a reader of veteran actor Una McLean playing the Wicked Queen in *Snow*

White there and singing 'Don't I Look Gorgeous In This?' Una looked down at a group of kiddies in the front row who were all giving her a thumbs down as she sang it, and she asked for the song to be taken out the show.

SAD news that the pop charts are not what they were. Now with downloads, instead of just singles, they include all songs from albums individually, so that Ed Sheeran has 15 of the top 20 tracks just now. Boring.

Anyway, we recall when Princess Beatrice cut Ed's face at a party while swinging a sword in a mock knighting ceremony. As stand-up Janey Godley commented: "If a Glasgow woman had a sword, the cops would have been called."

WHEN is a star not a star, asks Paul Drury, who explains: "Taxi driver brother-in-law tells me, 'Had one of those blokes from *River City* in the back of the cab once'. He only knew because the passenger mentioned he was an actor with a part in the popular BBC Scotland soap. 'Really?' said my brother-in-law. 'I've watched it a couple of times recently and I can't remember seeing you'. 'Aye,' replied the thespian. 'I've been in a coma for a while'."

SINGER Elvis Costello published his biography, *Unfaithful Music and Disappearing Ink*, a couple of months back.

Reader John Munro tells us: "Early on in the book he recalls the time he played at the Ayr Pavilion back in 1980.

"'Part of the audience disappeared through a hole in the floor that had collapsed under an onslaught of stomping and jumping that passed for dancing'.

"Ah, happy days."

THE BBC reports that singer Madonna is adopting a further two children from Malawi. A reader once told us years ago that he was in the Post Office when the assistant told him that he had offered a customer the choice of two Christmas stamps - either reindeer or Madonna with Child. "Aw, gie us Rudolf," the customer replied, "Ah cannae staun' that Madonna wumman, takin' thae weans away frae Africa."

TALKING of comedians, Aaron Bennett, who appeared at Glasgow's Stand Comedy Club last month, has been talking about living in London these days. As he put it: "My neighbourhood watch has just asked if I'd like to help in the fight against terrorism.

"Last week it was to stop people stealing bins."

RATHER than just talk about their books, crime writers Douglas Skelton, Michael Malone, Lucy Cameron and Caro Ramsay have devised a comedy whodunnit play, *Carry on Sleuthing*.

The elegant Caro got really into the play and took a lot of time drawing on a fake moustache the last time it was performed. A woman in the audience was heard telling her pal that Caro should really do something about her facial hair.

Says Caro: "Yet there was no mention of my hairy wart, which I made from breakfast cereal and cat fur."

HARRY POTTER author J.K. Rowling annoyed a few right-wingers in America by describing Donald Trump as a racist. One American contacted her on social media to say he would now burn his *Harry Potter* books and DVDs. Joanne merely replied: "Well, the fumes from the DVDs might be toxic and I've still got your money, so by all means borrow my lighter."

GOOD to see Mel Brooks getting a Bafta Fellowship at the age of 90. Mel served in the American Army during the war, and tells the story of taking a patrol out when they came across telephone polls with ceramic insulators and they had a shooting contest to see who could hit the most.

When they got back to base there was a flap about the telephone lines being down and fears that there were German snipers. So Mel took his patrol back out. "We never did find them," he said.

COLLEAGUE walks over and ignores the fact I'm trying to look very busy. He bellows: "The actor Daniel Radcliffe revealed he was 'dependent on alcohol' to make it through the final *Harry Potter* films.

"Makes two of us."

CELTIC Connections is Glasgow's big musical gathering in

January. Mike Ritchie tells us: "Aaron Lee Tasjan, in his support slot to Margo Price at Oran Mor earlier this week, told the audience, 'My surname is kinda weird. Just hope I'm pronouncing it right'.

"And, introducing his fine song, '12 Bar Blues', he explained, 'This is about drinking in twelve different bars, not a musical playing style'."

MUSIC festival Celtic Connections is going great in Glasgow just now. Irish fiddle star Martin Hayes, about to play 'The Star Of Munster', told his audience about one of his students who wanted to play the tune at a post-festival shindig. The student asked accordionist Jackie Daly of the great Patrick Street band if he knew 'The Star Of Munster'.

"Do I know it?" replied Jackie, not keen to be interrupted, "I am the f****** 'Star of Munster'."

MIKE Ritchie also tells us: "Fire alarm went off at the Royal Concert Hall on Saturday evening during a live broadcast by Celtic Music Radio of the Danny Kyle Open Stage event.

"As the crowd made to leave, final act The Deadly Winters asked show host Liz Clarke if they should keep on playing. To which the ever-genial Liz replied, 'It's no' the *Titanic*'."

THE Herald story that actor Samuel L Jackson will be in Scotland soon to film the next *Avengers* film reminds us of when he was in St Andrews to play in the Dunhill golf championship. He once explained about the sport: "I very seldom get angry at golf. The year I started golf I had a caddie and one day I did get angry with myself and threw a club. My caddie told me, 'You're not good enough to get mad'. I have never thrown a club since."

OUR American music contact Mike Ritchie tells us: "American musician, Dan Stuart, is never less than laconic. He posted on Facebook 'My New Year's resolutions are to bathe regularly and look for a girlfriend. Dunno, maybe one is related to the other'."

GLASGOW artist Alasdair Gray is to have his first exhibition in London. He told the BBC that it doesn't matter to him as much as it once would. It reminds us of when Alasdair was buttonholed at Oran Mor and told that his fantastic ceiling painting would be a "wonderful legacy to the people of Glasgow".

"I just did the colouring in," Alasdair replied.

EDINBURGH is getting ready for the annual cultural onslaught known as the Fringe. In a coffee shop Fiona Forshaw overhears two ladies discussing what shows they would like to attend. "I see there's one called *The Naked Magicians* - apparently they're from Australia," says one.

"They would be," replies her friend. "No-one in Edinburgh takes their cardigan off after 6pm".

ANDY Murray's mum Judy gets recognised when she's out and about. She described a recent encounter in Glasgow when a woman came up and said: "Can I get your autograph, hen?" "Sure," replied Judy. And afterwards: "Aw, you've got a lovely signature. You should see mine's. It's inedible."

FILMGOERS have been praising Christopher Nolan's film *Dunkirk*. Not so old Diary chum and former Radio Scotland presenter Tom Morton, who declared: "Of the many inconsistencies and anomalies in the movie *Dunkirk*, the 1960s/70s blue rail carriage upholstery annoyed me most."

COCKNEY stand-up Micky Flanagan is appearing at the Hydro in Glasgow tonight. He once remarked: "I was asked to go on the TV show *Who Do You Think You Are?* I told them that where I come from, that sounds like the start of a fight."

GREAT concert by The Who at Glasgow's Hydro at the weekend, with the audience being a little on the mature side for a rock concert. As Pete Townshend announced before one of their numbers: "This is one for the over-65s in the audience." He then went straight into their classic 'My Generation'.

THE news that arguably Glasgow's most famous painting, Salvador Dali's *Christ of St John of the Cross* is to go to London on loan reminds us of children's entertainer Mr Boom's meeting with Salvador.

Before he was Mr Boom, a young Andy Munro played in a jazz band in Catalonia, Spain, which was invited to play for Salvador

Dali. They weren't sure what to kick off with and Andy came up with the inspired suggestion of their own version of 'Hello Dolly', entitled 'Hello Dali'.

"He didn't get the joke," Andy later admitted.

SURVIVAL expert Ray Mears is to give a talk on surviving in the wild at Queen's Hall, Edinburgh, in October. We remember comedy writer Sanjeev Kohli once commenting: "Ray Mears reckons you can make a meal with whatever you find on your doorstep. So time to get creative with a still-warm beige fox's poo."

OUR tale about the band playing 'Hello Dali' to the famous painter reminds John Henderson: "Glasgow's Arnold Brown was the comedic warm-up act for Frank Sinatra at Ibrox Park in 1990.

"He says Frank asked before the show for some local insight and tips, and Arnold suggested in his laconic manner that Frank could perhaps address the Scottishness of the occasion by opening with 'Fly Me to Dunoon'. Frank demurred for some reason, he says."

A WORLD Fringe Day is taking place in July to mark the 70th anniversary of the Edinburgh Festival Fringe. What fun the performers have in Edinburgh. We remember Welsh stand-up Dan Mitchell saying he once had to spend the night on a park bench in Edinburgh during the Fringe as there was a mix-up over his accommodation. In the morning he woke to find a Rustlers microwaveable burger by his head. Said Dan: "My only problem was, if they thought I was homeless, where was I going to get a microwave?"

AFTER our mention of celebrity chef Heston Blumenthal, reader John Crawford remarks: "Heston and his quaint recipes - he serves 'twice and thrice cooked chips' as a delicacy. In the Garnock Valley in the 60s we called these 'reheats' and moaned if there were too many of them in a poke of chips."

THAT great Glasgow play *The Steamie* is 30 years old, and is being revived at the King's Theatre in Glasgow this October. When it was first performed by Wildcat, director Alex Norton explained to *The Herald* it was set in a wash-house. "Genuine props like scrubbing boards and sinks are there," said Alex who added: "It was too complicated to provide water as well, which is a pity as we could have got the company's laundry done at the same time."

SCOTS stand-up Craig Ferguson, former *Late Show* host on American television, is returning to the Edinburgh Fringe at the Gilded Balloon for the first time in 24 years.

Craig once told of a Glasgow gig where, when he got outside, someone shouted: "You were rubbish!" Craig went over to the guy who then told him that he had in fact been pretty good. When Craig asked him why he had shouted out he was rubbish, the chap replied: "Just to keep your feet on the ground."

DON'T really want to get into the *Doctor Who* debate so will just leave you with the comment of Jonny Sharples, who says: "Your dad thinks Doctor Who being a woman spoils the realism of someone travelling through space and time in a phonebox while fighting bins with plungers on them."

WE mentioned Billy Connolly's knighthood, and Bill Thomson in Glasgow observes: "Can you imagine the hilarious routine he would have created years ago about a working-class hero accepting a knighthood?"

IT would break your heart, the Scotland-England score, after two great goals from Celtic's Leigh Griffiths. As film actor Martin Compston later confessed: "Already watched the replay of those two free kicks by Griffiths considerably more times than my wedding video."

GREAT news for *Still Game* fans as writer Greg Hemphill

announces he has finished writing the new series. We recall Greg once saying that he and Ford Kiernan were filming *Still Game* in Maryhill when a local urchin tapped at their car window, crying: "Gauny geez an interview."

Greg was baffled until the youth added: "Geez an interview - it's fur ma sister." Greg pointed out that what he really meant was an autograph, adding wittily: "Unless your sister's Kirsty Wark."

The youth angrily replied: "Ma sister's never cursed her work - she's at Gregg's. They give her the bashed sausage rolls for nothin'."

A READER phones: "I guess we now know why the BBC chose the next Doctor Who to be a woman.

"She's cheaper."

SO Radio Scotland's boss Jeff Zycinski is quitting. We recall all those years ago when he took over and wanted programmes to be more appealing to younger listeners. Immediately, Gary Robertson had an on-air chat about Michael Jackson, but the effect was perhaps spoiled by the first caller announcing after a couple of minutes: "I'll have to go now, Gary, that's my home help arrived."

AND was it not former broadcaster Tom Morton who told of Jeff crossing the bridge to Pacific Quay with a BBC bigwig from down south who looked down into the Clyde and declared: "There's a dolphin! And there's a swan going towards it!" Jeff confided to Tom the dolphin was actually a bit of wood and the swan a plastic bag.

10
The Curse of the Drinking Classes

Well we spend a third of our lives there, so stories about work are bound to crop up, even though not everyone is happy when they reach their office or factory.

THE FIRST 5 DAYS
AFTER THE
WEEKEND ARE
THE HARDEST

THE news story about 15,000 people applying for 78 jobs as train drivers on the East Coast line reminds a reader of the NUR official called in by bosses who wanted to discipline a train driver who had called in sick and taken a day off.

They showed the union official a cutting from a weekly newspaper which reported that said driver was runner-up in a contest that day at his local golf club.

"The official looked at it, then told management: 'I bet he would have won it if he hadn't been sick.'"

A GLASGOW businessman tells us a colleague had returned from a business trip to London and complained that he found it difficult to get to sleep in his hotel room.

"Was it because the bed was too uncomfortable?" he asked.

"No," replied his colleague, "it was lying there knowing there was a whole Toblerone bar sitting there in the room's mini-bar."

THE *Herald* story that Bank of Scotland customers can take selfies in order to open an online account reminds Cameron Thomson in Strathaven: "When I was a young teller in a branch in Larkhall I was more than a little zealous when applying the rules. I was approached by a local worthy who wanted £10 from his savings account, and I insisted on asking for ID. This prompted the gentleman to turn to his pal in the queue behind him and say, 'Tell this wean who ahm ur' which brought a confirmation announcement of, 'Aye, it's him'.

"ID process complete, he got his tenner."

A WORKER in a Glasgow office said he was reading a poster on the wall about the company offering free flu jabs this winter. A colleague came up and told him: "You don't want that."

When our reader asked why not, he replied: "How can you phone up pretending to have flu if you've already taken their flu jab?"

WORKPLACE nicknames. Actor Jimmy Martin, who plays Eric in *Still Game*, reminds us of the worker at the old Singer sewing machine factory in Clydebank who was known as Chocolate Mint. His timekeeping was such that he always turned up after eight.

A READER phones to reminisce with us about his time working in a factory in Glasgow. He said he was always impressed by a colleague who had a poor attendance record, but didn't let it bother him. When he came in one day and his boss said to him: "You missed your shift yesterday," he merely replied: "Not particularly."

A READER on a south side train into Glasgow last week heard a young woman tell her pal that a workmate in her office was very competitive. As she put it: "She's the kind of person if I told her she was the Queen Bee in the office she would demand to know who was the Queen A."

WORKPLACE nicknames continued. Ian Forrest in Laurencekirk tells us that, when he was general manager of a food factory in Montrose, he would wear a red hard-hat while out on the factory floor and his chief engineer wore a blue one.

He later learned that the female workforce, who simply wore hairnets, referred to the pair as Swan Vestas and Bluebell - two leading brands of matches distinguished by the colour of the match-heads.

MALCOLM Boyd in Milngavie recalls: "When I worked at the British Leyland Albion plant in Scotstoun there was an employee who was known as 'Jehovah' because if any incident happened in the factory he was first on the scene to say that he had witnessed it."

Adds Malcolm: "A few years after I had left the Albion, it was bought over by the Dutch manufacturer Daf Trucks. I met one of my former colleagues who told me that the factory was being renamed. The new name - LayDaf."

NOMINATIVE determinism is the theory that some people gravitate towards jobs which reflect their names.

Clydebank farmer Stuart Christie thought that was fair enough when his banker was Sandra Ledger, but was slightly concerned when his accountant was David Cheetham and his lawyer was Stuart Clink.

A KILLEARN reader passes on: "Seen in Great Western Road, a glazier's van with the legend, 'Hendersons the Glaziers - we're only a stone's throw away'."

THE *Herald's* archive pictures of the Highland Light Infantry in Glasgow reminds veteran actor Jimmy Martin that when he lived in Partick, a neighbour who had been out of work for some time joined the HLI. The neighbour explained that many long-term unemployed folk were forced into joining, which give the HLI the nickname Helluva Long Idle.

ASH Wednesday yesterday with a reader telling us: "The stories about being late for work reminded me of the time I smeared ash from my fag end on my forehead and told my boss I was late as I was in church on Ash Wednesday. Has everyone not done that? "I'm going to Hell, amn't I?"

WE also recall an actual churchgoer on Ash Wednesday who was asked when she returned to her Glasgow office what the mark was on her forehead.

She replied it was ashes, and her colleague, not the brightest admittedly, asked who's funeral had she been to.

AND Ash Wednesday is of course the start of Lent, when you are supposed to give up something for 40 days. As one reader once cheerfully told us: "What do I give up for Lent? Usually my New Year's Resolutions."

AND tales about Lent remind Bob Stewart: "A meteorologist friend once delivered the daily weather forecast on a local radio morning show, and was then drawn into the general conversation by the presenters. When asked by them if he was giving up something for Lent, he replied, 'Chastity!'. His bosses were not amused and suspended him from the programme for several weeks."

OUR late-for-work stories remind Jim McGovern: "My attendance at work when I was an apprentice glazier could occasionally be erratic. I was offered Saturday morning overtime drilling mirrors in the workshop. I arrived around 8.15am a bit under the weather and the gaffer, looking none too chuffed, said, 'You should have been here at eight o' clock.' My stupid answer, 'Why? What happened?' got me sent home with four hours overtime down the pan."

GREAT night at the Oran Mor Whisky Awards in the West End last week where distillers were telling their favourite yarns. The one we liked was the distillery where the workers had discreetly fitted a small additional pipe that led to a tap outside the distillery where they could siphon off some of the nectar away from the eyes of customs.

All went well until there was a small fire on the premises and a customs man grabbed a pail, filled it at the tap and threw it on the fire only to watch in amazement as the flames suddenly enveloped the room.

LATECOMING continued. Says entertainer Andy Cameron: "I recall approaching Sir William Arrol's in the fifties and a wee wummin asking a group of us, 'Has the horn blew?' and Danny Irvine, the works' comic, informing her, 'Ah don't know whit colour the horn is hen'.

"And a certain Rangers legend was chastised by Walter Smith, 'McCoist, late again, you're fined a week's wages'. Super Ally was aghast. 'Och be fair gaffer' he moaned, 'this is the earliest ah've been late aw week'."

OUR job interview stories have really gone down memory lane as David Miller in Milngavie tells us: "Comedian Lex McLean once said he was being interviewed at the burroo and was asked if he had any views of work. 'Well,' he replied, 'our kitchen window looks into John Brown's yard'."

What do you mean old? We prefer the term classic.

WE are sent research claiming that the 4.22 am train from Glasgow Central to Manchester Airport is the train most likely to be cancelled on any train route in Britain. Can't help thinking there's a Scottish driver out there who doesn't like getting up at half-three in the morning.

COMPANIES it seems are cutting back on open-plan offices as they reach the conclusion that they are bad for productivity. A reader tells us that she was on the phone in her open-plan office to her teenage son who was not quite grasping her instructions.

When she hung up she heaved a sigh and said: "No-one ever listens to me." Immediately five co-workers shouted out: "We do."

ROBERT Jeffrey's just-published book on shipbuilding, *Giants of the Clyde*, tells of Murray Easton, the son of Yarrow's chairman Bob Easton, being employed in the yard as a ship manager, and trying to avoid claims of nepotism.

He was installed in a Portakabin as his office, and shortly afterwards some of the yard workers put a sign over the door, recalling a favourite hit of the time. The sign stated The House of the Rising Son".

WELL done the trade union Unison obtaining a court ruling that it was unlawful to charge punters big fees to pursue claims for unfair dismissal. We still recall the chap who worked as a salesman for car company Arnold Clark and was awarded more than £8,000 for unfair dismissal from the firm.

It was a real Nae Luck Award for Arnold Clark as their representative failed to turn up for the hearing - and later explained that he had suffered a puncture en route and was not carrying a spare.

OUR mention of nominative determinism - the suggestion that we are drawn to jobs that match our names - has reader John

Mulholland recalling: "Years ago I had to endure one of those leaving speeches from the boss as I had been promoted and was transferring to another office. 'Many of you will think that John's surname originated from Ireland,' he said. 'However, you are wrong: it is Dutch. I did some research into the name and I found that it means hard-working, diligent and conscientious.

"As for his forename, remarkably, I found that it translates as 'Isnae'."

RODDY Young was in a Partick pub where the staff were wondering where the new start was, as he had not turned up for his two-hour trial shift.

Says Roddy: "At 6.55pm, almost two hours late, he casually walked through the door protesting his innocence. 'I was asked to do a trial shift from five to seven', he insisted, which was a misunderstanding about what was meant by five to seven. I've not seen him since."

A GLASGOW reader emails: "I refused to believe my dad was stealing from his job as a road worker. But when I got home, all the signs were there."

BAD pun alert! After *The Herald* archive picture about the ropeworks in Port Glasgow, Jim Morrison recalled as a youngster visiting a ropeworks in Ibrox when he worked for ferry company CalMac. He then felt the need to add: "I was told about the school leaver who got a job at the Ibrox ropeworks, but he didn't last very long - he was caught skipping out early one afternoon."

WE mentioned Prince Philip's imminent retiral, and Sue Forsyth in Bearsden recalls: "When we lived in Windsor in the sixties my father was a part-time fireman. The brigade was called to a fire at Home Farm on the Windsor Castle Estate.

"To prevent it spreading the firemen climbed up and down a ladder removing bales of hay two at a time. Prince Philip came to help. He was then challenged as to why he was only carrying one hay bale instead of two. His reply was 'because you lot are being paid to do this and I am doing it for fun!'"

A GLASGOW reader swears to us he was in a city pub the other night when a younger chap came in to meet his pals and told them he had lost his new job as a waiter. When his concerned mates asked him what happened he told them: "The boss asked me if I could clear Table Five. I told him I hadn't tried the High Jump since school, but I would give it a go."

SAYS John Mulholland: "The story about the ropeworks reminded me of a tale told years ago about an underwear factory that was experiencing stock losses.

"The owner suspected theft and checked employees' bags but no undergarments were found. It was then decided to have spot checks on staff in case they were wearing multiple sets of underwear, but again, they were wrong.

"It was some time before they worked out that some staff were arriving with no underwear at all and were simply putting on some before they went home."

A READER emails to explain capitalism to us. "A boss bought a new BMW car, which one of his employees was admiring. So the boss said to him, 'Do you know, if you work hard, show up on time, never skive off early, work all the overtime I ask you to do...' At that the worker interrupted him, 'Do you mean I could get a car like that?' "But his boss replied, 'No I was going to say, 'then I'd be able to buy an even bigger BMW'."

OUR stories about job interviews remind a Glasgow reader: "I was once asked that clichéd question, 'What would you say is your greatest weakness?' I replied, 'Being unemployed'."

I KNEW it was a bad idea to look up when a colleague arrived at my desk. "Someone left a huge lump of Play-Doh in my living room," he announced.
"I don't know what to make of it."

FED up with these phone calls asking if you've had an accident? It reminds Jim Nicol in Lenzie: "In the Railways there was a daily incident log which recorded all occurrences of any note, and I recall an accident which did not get the sympathy it merited.
"It recorded an injury to a member of staff who had been

occupied splitting sets of coaches. The heading of the report was the problem, 'Shunter pulled muscle whilst doing the splits'."

AFTER our story about competitive colleagues, David Moncur in Brightons, near Falkirk, tells us: "I used to work with one such person who, if you told him you had been to Tenerife on holiday, he would claim to have gone to Elevenerife. "

AT last a colleague made me smile when he came over to tell me: "Been struggling with diarrhoea for nearly a week.
   "But finally I have worked out how to spell it."

JOB interviews, more of. Alistair Fraser says his father was paid off in the autumn of 1962 from his job as a pattern maker in a foundry in Stevenston. He and his mates went for an interview at the local buroo, only to be told there was no work for his trade but that things might pick up in the following spring. As he left, one of his pals asked him how he had got on. "That guy in there," he replied, "thinks I'm a daffodil."

I SWEAR a colleague, clearly a fan of the Jacksons, was lurking at my desk yesterday in the hope I would turn up as he immediately buttonholed me with: "I had a bet on three horses at the weekend. Sunshine, Moonlight, and Good Times. Not one winner. I blame it on the bookie," before walking off.

OUR story about the old Glasgow housing office in High Street reminds Willie Dickie in East Kilbride of working there as a teenager and being put on the public counter. Says Willie: "One of my first applicants was a wee Glasgow woman who said her husband couldn't be with her as he was 62. Yet the application form filled in a year earlier said he was 48. With that confident exuberance of youth I laid bare her deception.

"The exchanges became increasingly confusing until eventually her eyes lit up and she said pityingly, 'Oh son, that's not his age, that's his shift'."

11

I'll Drink to That

We never condone drinking to excess, but the pub is still the place where you can hear the funniest of yarns, tall tales and bad advice. Readers send us their favourites.

A READER in a Glasgow pub at the weekend heard a young customer tell a young woman he was chatting to: "Stick your tongue out and I can tell your personality from it." When she did in fact expose her tongue, the chap looked at it and told her: "Gullible."

AND talking of pubs, a reader swears to us he heard a young man in a Byres Road pub tell a woman that he was God's gift to women. "Only if God shops in Poundland," she replied.

THE pubs being busy just now reminds a veteran barman of his first shift in a Glasgow bar when he was asked for a "half and a half pint" which used to be a common tipple. He tells us: "I served the whisky, turned to pour the half pint, and when I took it over I couldn't see the customer. He had done a runner after drinking the whisky. From that day on I always served the beer first when asked for a half and a half."

A READER on a late-night bus in Glasgow heard a gently-swaying young woman argue with her pals: "But in dog wines I've only had one."

SOME deep subjects are discussed in Glasgow pubs. A reader heard a group of topers discuss whether they had ever thought of inventing anything. One of them piped up: "I once wrote to Pringles suggesting they put a twist mechanism like a stick deodorant in the bottom of their cans of crisps."

THERE is nothing like a trip to a Glasgow pub for some philosophy. A reader heard one toper in a city centre pub declare: "Do you know the best thing about women is how they can tell you what you really mean when you say something?"

A MERCHANT City reader was having lunch in a local pub where a chap at the next table dropped some food off his fork. The poor man's wife sitting opposite him shook her head, and declared: "Still, at least if you die they won't have to do a post mortem to find out what you had eaten - they'll just have to look at your shirt."

DISCUSSION in a Glasgow pub the other night involved a toper asking: "Why do the makers of microwaves not include a volume control? Why must I wake the wife when I come in late and want to heat the leftover pizza?"

A GLASGOW reader says he had to agree with the toper in his local bar at the weekend who opined: "People always say 'He died penniless', as if it's a bad thing. Sounds like good timing to me."

OUR pub jokes remind John Gilligan of when he owned The Cross Keys in Stevenston, Ayrshire: "A guy walked in and asked a worthy at the bar, 'gonna lend me a tenner?'. After asking three times and being ignored, he was helped by the barman who asked the worthy if he could at least reply. 'Reply to whit? Ah canna hear him', he said.

   "So the barman said, 'Well I can hear him clearly'. 'Good,' said the regular. 'You can lend him the tenner then'."

OUR old pub joke sparks off a great deal of reminiscing. Entertainer Andy Cameron keeps the theme going with: "A tall handsome guy walks into a pub in Maryhill and the blonde brassy barmaid is stunned. 'Haven't seen you in here before. Are you local?' 'Aye but ah've been away for 20 years' says the gorgeous one. 'Abroad?' asks Blondie. 'Naw ah was in jail' says the big hunk, 'Ah murdered ma wife'.

   "'Oh', she says, pauses for a minute, and then, 'So, on your own then?'"

THERE has been a big growth in craft beers being sold in pubs, particularly India Pale Ale. An Edinburgh reader emails us: "My grandfather tells me there was an old gag. Chap walks into a bar and says, 'Give me a beer'. 'Pale?' asks the barman. 'No, a glass will do fine', replies the drinker."

BEER brand Foster's has announced it has sold a million pints since becoming the official beer at Glasgow's Hydro stadium. It reminds us of the Australian who told us Foster's is not that popular in Australia despite the advertising and added: "We often wonder how they get cats to balance on top of an open can."

A WHISKY distillery is being planned for Leith near the Ocean Terminal shopping centre and close to the Royal Yacht *Britannia*. Ian Stirling, one of the partners in Port of Leith Distillery, read a comment online about it where a critic wrote: "More poison being manufactured and subsequently consumed by the weak of mind." He says he was so taken with it that he has promised to put it on a T-shirt to sell at the gift shop.

A GLASGOW reader was amused when he heard a young woman walking down the street after a drink or two in the city centre tell her pal: "Sorry that I got so mad and said all those things that I really meant."

SOMETIMES Glasgow's leisure industry still has a bit to go. A West End reader who works in the east of the city went with a few colleagues for an after-work refreshment locally, where she went to buy some white wine only to be told they had run out.

When she pointed out there was an off sales across the road, the barman called over a local worthy and told him to run across and purchase a bottle for him.

"What will I get," asked the old toper. "Any old s***," replied the barman in our reader's hearing.

WISE words from a woman meeting her pals in Glasgow's Corinthian Bar on Saturday night who told them: "The trouble with being punctual is that there is nobody there to appreciate it."

OUR story about the teenager being asked to prove his age at a Glasgow club reminds James Scott in Singapore: "I was waiting with friends to get into a pub in Dundee when the two young ladies in front of us were asked by the doorman, 'Have you any ID?' To which came the reply, 'Aboot whit?'"

THAT great nightclub owner, Donald MacLeod, was fulminating in *The Herald* yesterday about his legendary Garage in Glasgow being faced with a £100,000 rates bill increase.

It reminds us of the customer who once explained: "I was trying to get into the Garage on my 18th birthday. A friend had given me a toy dinosaur as a present, so when they asked if I had anything on me I shouldn't, I pulled Dino out and shouted: 'Rawr! I have a vicious man-eating lizard, does that count?' "They then asked if I had any ID to prove that I was over five."

A LENZIE reader tells us he was in his local at the weekend when the woman at the next table asked her boyfriend to scratch her back. Eventually he asked her: "Is that ok?" She merely replied with a terse, "Higher!" so the bold boyfriend couldn't resist putting on a high squeaky voice and asking again: "Is that ok?"

ARTHUR Frame in Lanark tells us: "At the golf club at the weekend discussing the new drink-driving limits, one member said he blames the new limit for his alcohol problems. He explained that previously he would have two pints then drive home. Now he has six pints and takes the bus."

WE always liked the true story of darts being banned in Glasgow pubs 50 years ago as the council said it encouraged gambling and violence. A keen darts fan at the time asked a Glasgow bailie why dominoes, which also encouraged gambling, was not similarly banned. "Have you ever heard of anyone being stabbed with a domino?" the bailie memorably replied.

A WEST End reader in a crowded bar off Byres Road at the weekend was half-listening to a chap trying to impress a woman at the bar. Our reader did smile though when the woman leaned forward, patted the chap on the back of his hand, and told him: "Oh sweetie. If you have to tell people you're an alpha male, you're not."

SAYS Neil Dunn: "The mention of the Paisley-based commercial radio station Q96 calls to mind the 'good old days' of the nineties. The studios, situated at the bottom of Lady Lane and next door to the Cellar Bar, often witnessed a certain presenter put on a long record when it was quiet and nip next door for a 'swift one' before anyone was any the wiser."

A READER swears he heard a chap in a Glasgow pub at the weekend tell his pals: "I told my wife that a husband is like a fine wine and that I'll get better with age. So she said she'd be happy to lock me in the cellar."

TODAY'S piece of whimsy comes from a reader who says: "It's a fact alcohol increases the size of your phone's send button by 80 per cent."

TALKING of clubs, it's nice to know that nicknames are keeping up with changes in society. We hear of a young group of clubbers in Glasgow whose pal David couldn't get into a club as he had lost his ID. They now call him Dav.

LESS than a fortnight to the start of the Edinburgh Festival. As Fringe stand-up Steff Todd mused at the weekend: "My mum always says, 'You won't find a husband in a nightclub'. But I'm in one now and there's loads of married men."

VERBAL misunderstandings continued. Says Mary Duncan: "I and some friends eating at a table in a booth when the waitress clearing the table asked me to pass her 'that bowl'. I said , 'Yes, of course - but there isn't a bowl on the table'. She replied, 'The sauce boa'le!'"

TODAY'S piece of whimsy comes from Phil Swales who points out: "In opera, the show isn't over until the fat lady sings.
   "In karaoke, it's just getting started."

IT was announced yesterday that the council has agreed to fund a £7 million improvement scheme for Sauchiehall Street in Glasgow. We have always found the thoroughfare very down to earth and recall the Sauchiehall Street pub that put a noticeboard outside which stated: "Quiz night - nae smart arses".

12

Shop Till You Drop

The other place people gather is shops, even though the internet is lessening the grip shops have on us. Here are a few of our readers' encounters while shopping

STILL cracking weather in Glasgow. A reader was in the Asda in Toryglen when a female shopper in front of her handed over a lady shaver with a security tag to the checkout assistant.

Says our reader: "The assistant couldn't remove it and passed it to a colleague who also struggled. Finally the customer told them, 'Come on girls. Sun's oot and I cannae have hairy legs'."

OUR bakery story reminded Tom Strang in Barrhead of his student days driving a van for Ascot Bakery in Greenock. Says Tom: "As the last customer left my van, a four-year-old boy jumped into the back and said, 'Mister, gies a bun'.

"When I asked if he had any money and he said no, I told him he couldn't have one. After a five second delay, the urchin said, 'Gies a bun mister or I'll fart in your van'.

"He duly got the bun."

TODAY'S piece of whimsy comes from Neil who writes: "Our local chippy's started using magazines instead of newspapers to wrap the suppers. I'm eating them out of *House and Home*."

GETTING old continued. Says Simon Holland: "Remember before Amazon reviews when you could just buy a toothbrush without six hours of research?"

TALKING of presents, those of you who like to buy online will agree with Aaron Fullerton's sentiments when he advises: "Before you buy that nice jacket online, ask yourself, 'Am I willing to delete one extra email every day for the rest of my life?'"

A READER at Silverburn shopping centre heard a chap looking at a display of watches tell his wife: "I can't think of any scenario where a watch that can work under 50 metres of water would be my main concern if I was 50 metres under water."

WE hear a woman in a Renfield Street bar confess to her pals: "Was in by myself on Saturday and ordered a pizza from Domino's. It was so big that I shouted 'Pizza's here!' into an empty room so the delivery boy wouldn't judge me."

A WHITECRAIGS reader was in a Glasgow clothes shop where the oleaginous assistant told a mother and daughter shopping together that they looked like twins. Our reader thought the mother was quite sharp in replying, "Well, we were separated at birth."

TALKING of Hallowe'en, a Bearsden reader on the bus into Glasgow heard a young chap heading to his supermarket shift tell his pal: "Whenever someone is buying a Hallowe'en costume I point at their face and ask if I've to charge them for the mask as well. No one's complained so far."

FED up with all those fake occasions that card sellers seem to dream up? Tim Fairs, at Clintons Cards, tells us this is Play The Recorder Month. But we forgive him as he goes on to explain: "The first recorder probably dates from mediaeval times and was excavated from a castle moat in Holland in 1940. Whether or not it was thrown into the moat by parents exasperated by their child's practice is anyone's guess."

He then added: "For those less enthusiastic about the sound of recorder practice, I'm told that Boots sell earplugs, and there's usually one near a Clintons store."

TODAY'S piece of whimsy comes from a reader who emails: "When one door closes, another one opens.

"That's the trouble with me thinking I could put an Ikea wardrobe together by myself."

TARTAN Day yesterday, apparently, which reminds us of the reader who was in a Paisley dress-hire shop when a family walked in, and the father, with a tattoo of a chap on a horse on his arm, declared: "Wur here fur a fittin' o' oor kilts." The assistant asked which tartan they required, and he replied: "Rangers tartan." Our reader admired the nerve of the assistant who then asked if it was for a wedding or a First Holy Communion.

READERS were recalling the old street traders, and Andy Cumming says: "I remember the old fruit shop in Candleriggs in Glasgow's Merchant City, and Harry Angus shouting, 'Two for a pound. Melons two for a pound'. I asked, 'How do you know when melons are ripe?' 'When they are two for a pound', said Harry."

STILL, it can be a tricky thing, shopping. Paul McElhone in Beckenham tells us about his wife and daughter going shopping for a pair of boots for the latter, who found a pair she liked but not in her size. The assistant said she would go to check the stock-room as a new delivery had just arrived, and the boots "were very popular".

At that his daughter's face fell and she asked her mother: "Does that mean they are common?"

AND let's face it, lots of men dislike going shopping. A South-side reader popped into a cheap and cheerful supermarket where he passed a disgruntled basket-carrier trailing behind his wife, quietly singing: "Strange beer to the left of me, cheap biscuits to the right.

"Here I am, stuck in the Lidl with you."

THE *Herald's* letters page has been holding a debate on cakes named after Scottish towns. Observes Norrie Christie: "No-one has mentioned the Ecclefechan Tart. A disincentive could be due to the locals' habit of dropping the prefix when referring to their village. Hence the tasty baked concoction of dried fruits in a pastry shell is colloquially known as a 'Fechan Tart'. I first became aware of the local custom when standing at a bus stop in Annan I was asked if the Fechan bus had been."

STREET traders continued as Brian Chrystal recalls: "I remember a trader at the Barras loudly flogging off assorted sizes of net curtaining.

He held up one piece, which he described as 'just the job for the bathroom windae', before turning to a group of female spectators and asking, 'Come on ladies - ony of youse got an inside toilet?'"

GOOD to see the Airdrie bakery being allowed to reopen after fears it could have been linked to an outbreak of hepatitis.

It somehow reminds us of the reader who heard a woman in a Greenock bakery ask for a loaf of brown bread, telling the chap at the counter: "I'm buying it for a visitor who is a broon breadie type.

"I prefer white. But as ma faither used to say, 'The whiter the breid, the sooner you're deid'."

RON McKenna's upbeat review of The Indian on Skirving Street - the restaurant's name - in *The Herald* reminds Malcolm Allan of when his father ran the premises in Shawlands as a chemist's shop.

Says Malcolm: "I would work there on Saturdays and I recall a lady (well, it would be a 'lady' as it was Southside) producing a bottle of a white antacid mixture which had been dispensed the previous day. She pointed to a black particle floating in the mixture and expressed her concern as to its identity.

"'Absolutely nothing to be worried about,' was my father's reassuring response after examining the bottle. 'That's simply a vitamin'."

OUR bakery tales remind Margaret Thomson: "Years ago, I bought an apple pie. On cutting it, I found a dead wasp. Took it back to the bakery, and the baker said, 'So that's where it went! We spent ages lookin' fur it!'"

STREET traders continued. Gordon Casely recalls: "Years ago at the Barras I watched two chaps selling bath towels. They started the prices high, and then came down to a mere pound for what they claimed was 100 per cent genuine Egyptian cotton. I felt I couldn't lose, so tentatively stuck my hand up. The lead trader must have seen the look of disbelief on my face, for he turned to his china and said, 'A towel to the gen'leman ower therr. And pit it in a poly bag tae keep the gen'lman's fingerprints aff the stolen property'."

HERE comes a colleague looking for me. "I heard Tesco were doing a mass giveaway of all the Fleetwood Mac albums," he declares, before adding: "But it was just *Rumours.*"

OUR mention of bakeries reminds Robin Gilmour of the Kilmarnock woman who returned to the shop with a roll she had bought to complain about a fly in it. The baker lent forward, plucked out the offending item, popped it in his mouth and said it was just a currant. We don't know of course whether it was a currant or whether the baker was willing to swallow a poor creature in order to save his reputation.

SOUTHSIDE reader Alan Stephen tells us a friend went to the aid of an aged shopper in the supermarket, walking slowly with a Zimmer frame, and asked him if he needed any help. Says Alan: "He took her to the wine section and asked if she could help carry his choice of four single litres of an inexpensive cider, and declared that 'It was better than a' they pills they gie ye'."

WE do like our pensioners on buses stories. Writer Deedee Cuddihy was on the bus from Glasgow to Dundee where she got chatting to a pensioner who told her about her pal who had become obsessed with checking the sell-by dates when doing her shopping.

She told Deedee: "I came across her in the supermarket last week, having an animated conversation with one of the shop assistants. I said, 'What's going on Jessie?' And she said, 'I'm just telling this young man that I can't find the sell-by date on this.' I asked what she was buying and she held up a pack of toilet rolls."

JOHN Bannerman, from Kilmaurs, was at a supermarket car park in Kilmarnock where a chap collecting trolleys was stopped by a pensioner who asked: "Can I get one of those trolleys?" Says

John: "With a straight face he simply replied, 'No you can't. I had to go and collect these 30 trolleys myself.' After a few seconds of disbelief on her face, all three of us burst out laughing. Good to see there is still a sense of humour in auld Killie."

OUR Glasgow shop with the "Nae dugs" sign reminds Foster Evans: "Renfrew stalwart and cobbler Bill Macguinness was sick of being asked to do bag repairs so he put a sign in his window stating 'No Bfag Repairs'. People would say to him, 'There is no F in bag repairs' and he'd reply, 'You're right'."

A READER was in a supermarket in Maryhill when he overheard a chap muttering, as he read the back of a packet: "Just tell me how many calories are in the entire package and save me the trouble of doing all the arithmetic."

TODAY'S daftness comes from Moose Allain, who says: "It always annoys me when a menu offers a nice crisp salad, and when it arrives there are no crisps in it."

WE'RE supposed to eat more fruit and veg it seems, and researchers have revealed that many folk cannot even identify common varieties.

Said researcher Simon Williams: "When asked to name 10 fruit and vegetables, one of the participants said, 'nine carrots and an apple'.

"Another insisted that celeriac was a fictional detective from Jersey."

We recall chef Andy Cumming visiting an east end supermarket where he took a couple of plum tomatoes and a handful of cherry tomatoes to the checkout.

The young chap at the till hesitated, and asked what varieties he had. Andy replied: "Plum and cherry."

"You're at it mate," he replied. "I know a tomato when I see it."

A PARTICK reader says she spent ages in her local shop trying to decide on a wee treat for herself before plumping for a 25p fudge bar. When she went up to pay, the store owner who had been watching her said: "I wish I had 20 customers like you."

She beamed at what she thought was an unexpected compliment until he added: "But unfortunately I have 200 customers like you."

SAD to see that sporting goods shop Greaves is closing its Sauchiehall Street branch, although the Gordon Street emporium will remain in business. We remember an assistant in the store being asked by a customer if he could borrow a football pump with a needle adaptor.

Not expecting a game to kick off in the store, she asked why he merely wished a temporary loan instead of a purchase, and he replied that he wished to clean out the wax in his hearing aid.

Alas, on that occasion his request fell on deaf ears.

OUR tales about Glasgow sports shop Greaves reminds David Muirie: "Years ago, when a hockey goalkeeper, I went to Greaves to buy a goalkeeper's box - a garment designed to protect the family jewels. I was somewhat nonplussed when the pretty young assistant asked what size I wanted. I replied, 'Large of course'. To which she responded, 'Sir, large is the smallest size we stock'."

A READER swears to us after our story about that great sports store Greaves closing their Sauchiehall Street branch that her pal went in there to buy table-tennis balls. When the assistant asked if she wanted practice balls or the higher-grade one-star or even three-star, she replied they were just for her cat to play with.

"How does it hold the bat?" the assistant immediately came back with.

INCIDENTALLY, boss Sandy Greaves once told us that after the great Spanish golfer Seve Ballesteros wore a Slazenger jumper with its famous panther motif, a female customer came in and asked Sandy: "Sees us wan o' they sweaters wi' the jumpin' dug."

WELL have you ever done this? Ross Craig muses: "You know when you still have half a tank but buy petrol to mask that you've failed to find the right way out of the supermarket car park?"

FOLK have been reminiscing about the Glasgow clothes shop Flip in Queen Street in the 1980s that brought in loads of second-hand authentic American gear. As broadcaster Nicola Meighan recalled: "I loved going to Flip when I was at school. One pair of old Levis I bought had a full set of false teeth in the back pocket."

FUNNY the things that become hot political issues. Minister Liam Fox was embroiled in an argument about whether the United States should be allowed to sell chlorine-washed chicken in Britain which is currently banned in the EU. As Jim in Troon commented: "I'm sure even Gary Lineker would have a struggle marketing Bleached Chicken flavoured crisps."

TODAY'S piece of whimsy comes from a reader who asks: "Am I the only person to be bothered that the patient in the game *Operation* is clearly wide awake?"

A READER passes on that she was in a Partick charity shop where a couple of elderly English ladies came in and were perusing the knick-knacks on the shelf. One of them handed an elaborate cup and saucer to her pal and asked her if she thought it was 19th century. "Don't think so, dear," she replied. "It says on the bottom 'dishwasher safe'."

A READER in a busy Glasgow pub garden yesterday heard the chap at the next table tell his pals: "One day I'd like to be wealthy enough not to check out the furniture folk have left on the pavement for the binmen."

OH dear, a colleague sees I'm at my desk and bears down on me. "I ordered stuff online and stupidly used my donor card instead of my debit card," he tells me. "Cost me an arm and a leg."

TODAY'S piece of daftness comes from Neil who says: "Cleanliness is next to godliness. That's the last time I buy a dictionary from the pound shop."

TRIED to slip out of the office undisturbed, but a colleague trapped me. "Had enough of my wife's little games," he declared. "Don't know why she has to buy the travel edition of everything."

13

Humour by Degree

Glasgow is becoming even more a university city, as degree courses multiply and student flats shoot up everywhere it seems. Very important stuff this degree malarkey but students do make us laugh.

LOTS of teenagers discussing their university options with their parents just now. Says one Hyndland reader: "Our son was adamant that he could look after himself if he moved into a flat when he went to uni. He then spoiled his own argument by accidentally biting his own finger when eating some chips from the McDonald's drive-in."

A GLASGOW reader tells us he heard a student type in Byres Road explain to his pal: "A good way to impress girls is to throw some Latin phrases into your conversation. At least, that's my modus operandi."

MORE on bringing up teenagers as a Newton Mearns reader phones to ask: "If, as Albert Einstein once said, insanity is doing the same thing over and over again and expecting different results, should I just stop cleaning my children's rooms until they've gone off to university?"

TALKING of students, we were asked the other day by one: "Where can I get a dozen spiders, mice droppings, and a pool of cat pee?" When we asked what for, she replied: "I'm moving next week and my landlord says I must leave flat in the condition in which I found it."

CONGRATULATIONS on the Royal Conservatoire of Scotland being named as the third best college of performing arts in the world. We know how arty it is by the fact it is only place we have seen a unicycle in the bike rack.

Anyway we are reminded of the student who recently borrowed a vinyl LP from the Conservatoire's library and took it back to ask why it only contained half the music it was supposed to.

The librarian took great delight in showing the young student that you can flip an LP over and play the other side as well.

WELL are your teenage children getting ready to go off to university this year? We liked the comment of a young woman named Erin who summed up her first taste of uni: "If you ever wondered what living in student halls was like, my housemates unfriended me on Facebook because I told them to take the bins out."

WE asked for your new students' stories. A West End reader was in a Byres Road bar at the weekend when three new students came in and ordered a round of drinks, with one proffering a £10 note to the barman. The server, who had rung up £11.50 on the till behind him, looked at the £10 note and told him: "You're no' in the Students' Union now pal."

WE mentioned students arriving at university last week and a reader in Glasgow's West End swears to us she heard one student in Byres Road confide to a pal: "We couldn't work out how to set the clock in the microwave. Eventually we just waited up till midnight and plugged it in exactly then."

ST Andrews University is runner-up in a poll of best British universities.

It reminds us of St Andrews having a reputation of being a bit posh, and a Glasgow father in town for his daughter's graduation couldn't get over the sign in the uni car park which stated "Four spaces reserved for Bentleys".

He was ranting about it later in a town pub when it was gently pointed out to him that the hall was being renovated by a Dundee firm of shopfitters called Bentleys.

A READER hears a student on Byres Road telling his mate: "It's funny, but I left a door open in the house the other day and my mum asked if I was born in a barn. I told her that seemed an odd question for, if anyone should know where I was born, you'd think it would be her."

OUR story about students reminded a Milngavie reader of his time years ago at Glasgow Yoonie when his class handed in essays and their professor reminded them that they should not have got anyone to help them write it.

One smart Alec declared that he had prayed to God before writing it, so did that count.

The professor merely replied: "I've had a quick glance at it. Trust me, he didn't help you."

A DESPAIRING Bearsden mother tells us: "When I do my teenage son's ironing I put it at the bottom of the stairs for him to take to his bedroom. For days he seems quite happy to step over the pile as if I had simply created an obstacle course to make his trips upstairs more interesting."

A HILLHEAD reader heard a student on Byres Road tell his pal: "I suppose like many people I used to daydream about being famous. But after what happened to famous people last year I'm quite happy to just be ordinary."

A READER in Byres Road overheard a student, now an expert on matters domestic seemingly, telling his pal: "The proper amount of time for a pan to soak before cleaning it is until you need to use it again."

WE mentioned Ian Spring's book *Real Glasgow* and just thought we should add a comment in it from Glaswegian filmmaker May Miles Thomas who was not impressed by the abilities of contemporary art students. Or as May memorably put it: "They couldn't draw their airse along the floor."

14
Laughter as Medicine

Keeping fit and healthy can sometimes be a laughing matter. And it can be scary going into hospital, so many people cope with humour, and then tell us about it.

THE National Health Service - it's great and we won't hear a word against it. However a reader in Ayrshire tells us a chap at his golf club was recounting the other day: "I had a small operation for an enlarged prostate. I was taken in as a day patient and was home that night. I wouldn't mind if it wasn't for the fact my dog had a similar operation and the vet insisted on keeping him in overnight."

AND that reminds us of the patient at A&E in Glasgow who was put on a heart monitor after complaining of chest pains. When the doctor arrived at his cubicle and asked if he smoked, the patient replied that he had given up.

"How long ago?" asked the doctor.

"Half an hour," replied the patient.

A READER was at his golf club in Ayrshire yesterday when a fellow player remarked: "I was at the doc's where he gave me some new medicine and told me not to take the pills on an empty stomach. He then looked at my stomach and added, 'Not that that's likely in your case'."

A MILNGAVIE reader heard a woman of a certain age in a coffee shop tell her pal: "My husband suggested I should tone down getting Botox injections. I scowled at him. Well, I tried to."

FOR some reason it was World Porridge Day yesterday. It reminds us of a reader who was a nurse in the Beatson and had to deal with an irate nun complaining about a patient marked as an RC on the ward noticeboard but who was unhappy with a visit from the nun.

Our nurse had to explain that P beside a name meant porridge had been requested for breakfast, C was cornflakes, and RC was Rice Krispies.

A PARTICK reader says he heard some young women discussing their fitness levels the other day when one of them declared: "My current fitness level is putting the hairdryer down after five minutes because it's too heavy."

GROWING old continued. Posits Simon Caine: "Laughter is the best medicine. Unless you've got a weak bladder. Then it's probably the worst thing imaginable."

ROOM for a daft gag as a reader emails: "Hello everyone, welcome to Plastic Surgery Addicts Anonymous.

"I see a lot of new faces here tonight."

WE overhear a chap in a Glasgow pub admit to his pals: "I know I shouldn't have, but I couldn't resist it." He added: "The wife came back from the doc's and said the reason she was feeling dizzy was because her iron levels were low.

"So I said, 'Would it help if I raised the ironing board?'"

THE middle of February is when membership of slimming clubs dips a little after the New Year surge. We remember the woman who recorded an increase in weight at her club in Glasgow and, when asked what had caused it, said her hamster had died.

When she was asked if that had sparked off some comfort eating, she replied no, but she had been forced to finish a large box of Milk Tray as she needed the empty box to bury Whiskers.

A GLASGOW reader heard a colleague ask another if they did any physical exercise to keep fit.

"Does shaking the vending machine when your Kit-Kat sticks count?" she replied.

OUR hospital story reminded John Crawford: "A friend who was due to have an endoscopy and a colonoscopy at the same time in hospital was asked by the doctor if he had any questions. 'Aye,' he said. 'If ye need tae use the same tube, can ye dae the endoscopy first please?'"

A COLLEAGUE comes over to tell us: "Got a call from a mate who said he was organising some five-a-side football and would I like to make up the numbers.

"So I suggested fliver hundrood and saxty clang."

IT'S terrible when even colleagues make fun of the Scottish diet. "I've got an exam question for you," bellows a fellow journalist with too much time on his hands. "If Tracey buys three apples, two oranges and a banana, how far south of Scotland is she?"

VERBAL misunderstandings continued, as taxi driver Brian Higgins tells us of waiting with other drivers for the Transplant Team at Glasgow's Royal Infirmary to finish their sterling work. Says Brian: "The call came through, 'First car on the rank pick up a doctor and take them home on account. Next car, ditto.' "Shortly afterwards the second driver entered reception and called out, 'Taxi for Dr Ditto'."

AH yes, the healthy eating message. A West End reader says he heard a young chap on the bus at the weekend tell his pal: "I'm so hungry I could eat vegetables."

GROWING old, continued. A reader heard a chap in his golf club announce: "My doctor told me exercise would add years to my life. It's true. I tried a jog around the estate and came back feeling like I was 80."

VERBAL misunderstandings continued, as Brian Johnston in Torrance says: "When I worked for the NHS, another staff member swore blind that a young doctor, not conversant with the local dialect, asked a patient if he was on any drugs or medication. On hearing the chap's reply, he then spent some time looking through pharmaceutical directories for information on the drug 'Amaframol'."

OUR tales of elderly golfers brings the claim from entertainer Andy Cameron: "After a hip operation I reckon I'm five weeks away from returning to the golf course, and I have a goal - I want to shoot my age, 76.

"Shouldn't take me long.... nine holes I reckon."

And Andy couldn't help adding: "Talking of the hip replacement, I recommend the NHS. They give you the old one home for the dug!"

COMEDIAN Johnny Mac, a stalwart of the Pavilion pantos, is joining Elaine C. Smith at the King's Theatre panto this year. We liked his observation the other week: "Pure Gym, Charing Cross, Glasgow, should be called, 'We let people come in and sit on gym equipment and look at their phones'.

"Maybe not as catchy."

FIRST world problems. John Morrison passes on the latest from the BBC, which reports: "Avocados should carry warning labels following a rise in knife injuries from cutting into the fruit, a doctor has warned.

Leading plastic surgeon Simon Eccles has said he treats about four patients a week at Chelsea and Westminster hospital for such wounds, with staff dubbing the injury, 'avocado hand'."

More of a problem in Chelsea than Wishaw General, we suspect.

A READER swears he heard a young woman in a Glasgow

pub tell her pal: "The pregnancy test confirmed my worst fears. "I'm just fat. "

A GLASGOW reader who had a mole removed was given a Greater Glasgow NHS information leaflet afterwards that states: "You should avoid a lot of alcohol for 24 hours after your procedure as it can cause more bleeding."

She tells us: "Is it only in Glasgow that they would put 'a lot of alcohol' rather than just 'alcohol'?"

A READER using a lift in a Glasgow city centre hotel watched as a fellow guest was running towards it, but the chap standing beside the buttons failed to press the one to keep the door open. As the lift took off, the chap turned to our reader and said: "If I could run that fast I'd be happy to use the stairs."

THE growing concerns that foreign doctors are leaving the NHS because of Brexit reminds us of the Ayrshire reader who swears a newly arrived Australian doctor at Crosshouse Hospital looked at a patient's notes which stated he lived in squalor and cheerfully asked: "Tell me mate, I'm new to these parts - is that far from Kilmarnock?"

WE mentioned bus conversations with pensioners using their free pass, and a Glasgow reader says: "Took a trip to Dundee and sat beside a retired nursing auxiliary who had worked the night shift at Ruchill Hospital where, she told me, they used to film the occasional episode of *Taggart*, and also the BBC medical drama *Cardiac Arrest*.

She said one night she arrived for work to find police vehicles in the car park and assumed filming was taking place.

"Not so - it turned out that a patient using oxygen had persuaded one of his visitors to slip him a pack of fags and a lighter and, on sparking up an illicit ciggie, had set the place on fire."

AN AYRSHIRE reader was discussing keeping fit at his local golf club where an older member declared: "The first time I see a jogger smiling, then I'll think about jogging."

IT'S tough at times drinking what is good for you. A Hyndland reader emails: "Drinking wheatgrass juice is a great way to know what being a lawnmower tastes like."

AN Ayrshire reader tells us he was in his golf club bar when a younger player was talking enthusiastically about his fitness regime. As he left the bar, an older member further along commented: "The last time I burned a thousand calories was when I forgot to keep an eye on the steak pie in the oven."

A READER swears to us that he heard a woman in the West End tell her pals: "It was ghastly. Shelf upon shelf without a vegetable on it."

When her pal asked: "Because of the bad weather?" she replied: "No, just a normal day in the shop near my office in Coatbridge."

HOSPITAL tales continued. Says John Mair: "I visited a hospital maintenance department that had on display a terse report submitted by an engineer. It read, '1.30am received call from Ward 3 complaining of sound of Radio 1 coming from heating system. This was keeping the patients awake and would affect their recovery. Left a warm bed, battled through a blizzard, arrived in ward at 2.15am. All patients asleep, could not hear any sound from heating due to patients snoring. Eventually found the problem to be a portable radio that had fallen behind a radiator.

"'Resisted temptation to turn up volume and replace behind radiator. Slammed radio down on nurses' desk and left ward at 2.30am. Outside the blizzard was blowing stronger. Spent rest of night huddled in porters' lodge'."

THE news that there is a courgette shortage due to a poor harvest in Spain reminds a reader of the class of first-year pupils in Glasgow being given a sex education lesson by a nurse. She held up a condom and asked what it was. Everyone in the class knew. She then took out a courgette to show how to apply said condom and someone asked: "What's that?"

HOSPITALS continued. Says Gordon Casely: "Some years ago, while enjoying the hospitality of Aberdeen Royal Infirmary, I couldn't help noticing that four ward-mates departed late every afternoon. When they returned in time for the evening meal, they looked a lot happier.

"The blighters had the habit of phoning a taxi, hopping aboard in their dressing gowns, then going a mile uphill to Murdo's Bar in nearby Cairncry."

GLASGOW'S planning officials have given their backing to Glasgow University to knock down much of the old Western Infirmary in the West End. We remember in the staff newspaper, former Western workers were trying to recall the name of the superintendent who patrolled the wards at night with her giant Alsatian dog. Someone at least could remember the dog's name and wrote to the newsletter: "Officially, it was Rufus. To drunks on the wards it was known as 'Keep that dug aff ma neck!'"

OUR tales of the old Western Infirmary in Glasgow remind retired surgeon David Knight: "They brought back fond memories of when I was a junior house officer there in 1975. A standout was the casualty porters who carried out triage years before this was introduced formally by A&E trained nurses.

"When a punter presented at the porters' window, the porter would allocate them to an appropriate speciality thus: arms and legs = orthopaedics, naughty bits = gynaecology (female) urology (male), stomach = surgical, everything else = medical.
"I don't recall them ever getting it wrong."

OUR favourite Western Infirmary story was when Celtic player Bobby Lennox was interviewed there after being stretchered off in an Old Firm game with a broken leg following a bruising tackle from Rangers captain John Greig. Propped up in the Western that evening with his leg in plaster, Bobby was being interviewed for *Scotsport* when the reporter asked him when he realised his leg was broken.

"When I saw John Greig running towards me," Bobby replied.

READERS continue to help us with stories about the old Western Infirmary. Says Fiona Black: "My sister was a student nurse in the Western in the 1950s when she had suspected appendicitis. An eminent surgeon came to examine her and she blurted out that they had had a lecture on the appendix, and she didn't think the pain was in the right place. 'Indeed,' he said courteously, and pressed an immaculately manicured finger on the spot. When she had stopped screaming he patted her hand and said kindly, 'and that, nurse, is why I earn approximately 10 times as much as you'."

OUR tales of porters performing crude triage reminds Stewart McCormick: "I was a junior house officer in the Western in 1968. While the porters generally managed to send punters appearing at the front desk to the correct department, on one occasion I was sent, as the receiving surgeon, a young man with severe abdominal pain. It took me only a few seconds to discover that his pain was in fact due to severe sunburn as he had spent several hours lying with his 'tap aff' in Kelvingrove Park."

OUR stories about the old Western Infirmary are turning into a *Carry On* film, as a retired nurse on Arran tells us: "I was a nurse at the Western in 1961 when a doctor climbed a ladder into my room. The night nurse and a porter arrived to say someone reported hearing male voices. I said I was listening to the radio, and they looked around the room.

"The next day the porter said I was lucky the night nurse didn't look in the wardrobe mirror as she would have seen the doctor under the bed."

AND Paul O'Sullivan recalls when Western staff drank in The Aragon in Byres Road. Says Paul: "One evening I was standing at the bar when the stereotype Glasgow drunk engaged us in conversation. 'See that sister ah mine? Driving me nuts. Keeps saying the da's going tae die and ah have tae phone the doctor. He's no gonnae die, ah can tell. Ah work over in the Western'.

"After a pause he says, 'Okay, ah work in the boiler-room, but after a few years ye pick these things up'."

SOMEHOW we got on to leaving bodies for medical research. As John Henderson tells us: "I made arrangements years ago for my body to be left to medical science - the only problem was explaining this to the rest of my devout Church of Scotland family, especially my parents. I explained this was a good thing, as I would be the first member of the family to successfully get into medical school."

IAN Gibson in Newtonmore wishes to open out the conversation to take in all hospitals and tells us: "When I worked at Edinburgh Royal Infirmary in the 80s, a porter with many years service was in serious trouble for some repeated misdemeanours. I received a full and heartfelt testimonial in his defence from a very senior medic which was quite unusual.

"On asking why, I was told that the medic was one of the pair discovered in flagrante on a snooker table in the junior staff quarters 30 years before. The porter was the one who had walked in on him."

AND it also allowed Alan Barlow in Paisley to recount the old gag: "There was the guy in the pub who bragged that his brother was in the medical department of the university. When asked what he did there the chap replied, 'He's in a big jar on a shelf somewhere'."

HOSPITAL misunderstandings continued. Brian Johnston in Torrance says the conference room at the hospital where he worked was being used to hold interviews for an orthopaedic surgeon, and reception staff were given a copy of the timetable and asked to show folk in.

Says Brian: "The ethnic diversity of the candidates was reflected by the names on the list. Eventually a receptionist reported that the second interviewee had arrived but, unfortunately, the first, a certain 'P'nel Con-veh-nez,' had failed to make an appearance. Above the list of names and interview times was 'Panel Convenes 09:30'."

TALKING of doctors, Rob Smith tells us: "I read with interest your comment on the Scottish terms being used by patients.

"It reminded me of a young patient who consulted me.

"When asked what his problem was he said, 'Ma hingmy's a' hingmied.'

"On examination I was able to confirm that his hingmy was hingmied and a successful operation dehingmied his hingmy."

WE mentioned those Fitbit things smug folk wear on their wrists telling them how much exercise they've completed. We spotted someone asking on an online forum: "Are you supposed to wear a Fitbit in a shower?" They then added: "I'm looking to break this thing as soon as possible and I need some advice."

AN interesting point from Chris Ide in Waterfoot after our medical tales who says: "In 1968, I travelled to Dundee to begin my medical studies. I was amazed by the ability of Dundonians to describe dramatic changes in their health and wellbeing by simply swapping two consecutive words in a sentence.

"Thus, if a patient said 'I'm no' awffy weel', that implied they were merely feeling a bit under the weather. By contrast 'I'm awffy no' weel' meant that they believed that they were at death's door."

WE also mentioned hospital radio, and Norrie Christie felt the need to remind us: "There was the fellow who was in hospital having his toes amputated due to severe frostbite. He was an Al Jolson fan and put in a request for any song by his favourite artiste. Unknowingly, the DJ played, 'Toot, toot tootsie, goodbye."

THE office is quiet on Fair Monday so there is nowhere to hide. A colleague tracks me down and declares: "I went to my local library the other day and asked where I could find a book on childbirth." I just stare at him but he continues anyway: "The librarian said, 'Try over there in the C Section'."

15
Senior Moments

It happens to us all of course, growing old. It can lead to aches and pains, forgetfulness, but hopefully a few laughs as well.

A READER gets in touch with the news: "According to a recent report, British men between 55 and 65, will, on average, have sex two to three times per week. Japanese men in the same age group, will have sex only once or twice per year.

"This has come as very upsetting news to most of my friends - they had no idea they were Japanese."

AN Ayrshire reader at his golf club heard one of the senior members declare: "I remember when you just referred to your knees as right and left - not good and bad. These were good times."

TAKING advantage of the mild December weather, an Ayrshire reader strolled into his golf club for a round where he heard a fellow member opine: "I read that the average person has sex 60 times a year.

"So I guess I'm going to have a helluva week this week."

RESEARCH by bathroom company Geberit shows half of all Glaswegians wake up at least once a night to use the toilet, taking longer to get back to sleep than anywhere else.

It, of course, reminds us of the two old timers complaining about having to get up every night to pee. Their pal chipped in: "I sleep through the night and never pee before eight in the morning." Then he added: "Trouble is, I don't wake up 'til half eight."

GROWING old continued. Says a Hillhead reader: "When I used to say, 'Last night was a bit of a blur' it meant I had drunk too much. Now it means that I had forgotten to take my glasses.

"I NEVER realised when I was younger," said the member of an Ayrshire golf club the other day, "that the nursery rhyme 'Head, shoulders, knees and toes' was simply a list of what would give you bother once you hit retirement age."

OUR tales of dodgy old drivers remind Ron Beaton of the classic tale: "My late father-in-law was a constant worry to his family each time he ventured out on the road. He owned a driving licence before tests became mandatory.

"On one trip from Dunblane to Ayr, he got lost somewhere in Glasgow and ended up in Bearsden. When questioned about the detour, he advised that he had decided to follow a taxi.

"When asked by the family why he did that he replied, 'I thought he would know where he was going'."

WE wanted to mention singer Vera Lynn's 100th birthday, so blame Phil Swales who declares: "What is Vera Lynn having for her birthday dinner? "Whale meat, again."

WE apologised for our daft gag about Vera Lynn on her 100th birthday, but somehow it didn't stop Andy Cameron from telling us: "Delighted to see that Dame Vera Lynn celebrated her century with a nice cake and champagne... unlike my Great Aunt Isa who unfortunately died on the very day she reached 100 years of age.

"So sad. We were only half way through giving her 'the dumps' at the time."

OUR story about old drivers reminds George Marshall in Glasgow: "My parents live in a small village in Ayrshire where an eccentric old couple used to drive to church in a bright yellow VW Beetle. In his later years the husband's eyesight was failing so badly that his wife had to give him directions and warn of obstacles en route.

"It made for quite a sight as the car rolled though the village at a blistering five miles an hour. Mind you, it gave you plenty time to get off the road before they came past."

GETTING old continued. A reader passes on the comment from American actress Ruth Buzzi: "My last birthday has done wonders for me. Wonder where I left my keys, wonder why it's so hard to get up, wonder why my joints crackle."

SO you think the bands you liked were so cutting edge, and then you realise your kids haven't a clue who you are going on about. Stephen Miller passes on a conversation from the touchline of a schools rugby match as one dad remarks: "It's terrible. My son doesn't know who the Ramones were."

"Weren't they the people who voted against Brexit?" says a second dad. "No, they built all the roads," chipped in a third.

THERE are some benefits to getting older. As reader Alex Mulholland tells us: "I went into a cupboard and discovered a bottle of Glenmorangie that I thought I had drunk at Christmas - so that's a benefit of becoming forgetful."

A GLASGOW reader tells us he was upset when he phoned an insurance company seeking life insurance but when he rhymed off his various medical conditions they told him, sorry, but he did not qualify.

He was even more upset when a different representative of the insurance company phoned him back a few days later and tried to sell him some funeral expenses cover.

"TRAVELLING into Glasgow by bus," says Donald Grant in Paisley, "I heard two grannies discuss their grandchildren. One said that she had told her grandson that he would have to stand nearer to the toilet bowl to avoid making a mess. When the wee boy had said, 'But I thought I was near enough Granny' she had sighed and replied, 'So does your Grandpa'."

TODAY'S piece of whimsy comes from a reader who says: "I found a jar of chilli powder in the cupboard that said on the side

'Best before 2015' and I thought to myself, 'Weren't we all?' so used it anyway."

GETTING old continued. A reader in Partick tells us: "I'm actually looking forward to being at that age where no one stops you if you take a supermarket trolley all the way home."

OUR mention of TV's *University Challenge* reminds Eric Flack in Drumchapel: "Many years ago I went with my mother to a recording in Glasgow as a relative was a 'reserve' and we had two passes. The BBC floor crew were fussing about telling the audience the dos and don'ts of filming when my mother got excited at recognising someone and exclaimed, 'There's that Bastard Gargoyne!'

"The floor crew person beside her muttered, 'Yes he can be'."

DAVID Donaldson says: "You know you're old when your granddaughter asks what a stationery shop is and the explanation that it was a place that sold Quink, foolscap paper, carbon paper and manila envelopes doesn't help much."

MANY people are concerned about the government announcing a change in the date that people qualify for their pension.

As Jonathan Haynes ruefully comments: "By the time I get to pensionable age it will be calculated by the formula: State Pension age = n+1, where n is my age."

GROWING old continued. Confides a Milngavie reader: "I was

on the phone to a pal when he suddenly said, 'What's up? Were you being sick?' I explained it was simply the noise I now make when going from standing up to sitting down."

WE asked about growing old, and an Ayrshire reader emails: "As a grown-up I'm not eating nearly as much ice cream as the 10-year-old me thought I would."

SAYS an Ayrshire reader: "Chap in the golf club is retiring next week. I asked him what he was going to do with his time. He told me, 'Get up early in the morning and drive around really slowly making everyone late for work'."

OLDER golfers continued. Jimmy Martin was passing the Musselburgh Links course when he asked a senior citizen coming off if he had had a good game. "Not yet!" he cheerily replied.

A READER heard a chap in the pub declare: "When I was a kid, I thought 50 was really really old. And now I'm 50 I've discovered I was right."

GROWING old continued. A Milngavie reader passes on: "I had a great round of golf at the weekend and was thinking as I drove home afterwards that I was doing really great for my age.

"I then struggled to get out of the car as I'd forgotten to unclip my seat-belt."

SAYS a Newton Mearns reader: "I motioned to my teenage daughter with my hand to wind down her car window. She looked at my hand gesture and told me, 'You do realise it's over 30 years since they invented electric windows?'"

16
Broadening the Mind

Travel introduces you to new cultures and also lets those from abroad see what Scotland is like. And it can be funny.

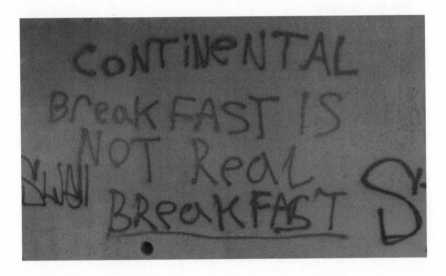

A MILNGAVIE reader just back from a cruise says he heard a woman from Glasgow at the next table say to her husband:

"That's the fourth time you've been up at the buffet. Are you not embarrassed what folk must think about you?" "Not at all," he replied. "I just tell folk I'm filling up your plate for you."

YES, it's Fair Monday today. Our mention of the Fair brings forth from a reader in Bishopbriggs: "It's not really a family holiday until someone in the car threatens to throw someone's else prized possession out of the window."

SEA LIFE in Blackpool is inviting folk on Face Your Fears Day to spend time with its sharks.

It reminds us of the Australian surfer going into a bar in Sydney and announcing he had been attacked by a Great White.

"Did you punch it on the nose?" asked someone further up the bar.

"No," replied the surfer. "He just attacked me for no reason."

AN American visiting Scotland this summer asked folk on the holiday website TripAdvisor what clothing he should pack for Scotland. A fellow tourist, from Canada, replied: "We were in Scotland for two weeks in late July. There were a couple of days when we were in Pitlochry that I would have worn shorts if I had them and there were a couple of days on Skye that I would have worn a pair of gloves if I'd had them."

MANY folk who go abroad on holiday get themselves a tattoo after injudicious amounts of alcohol. We are trying to verify the story that a young Glasgow lad on a Greek island heard the tattooist working on his back declare: "Eagle? I thought you said beagle."

READERS continue to arrive home from their holidays, and a Mount Florida reader confesses: "In films it takes anyone who breaks into a car 10 seconds to hot-wire it and drive away.

"Yet in Portugal last week it took me nearly 15 minutes to find the switch that opened the flap over the petrol tank."

MORE on the Fair holiday as a Motherwell reader tells us he was on holiday in the South of France one Fair when there was a white-faced mime artist performing on the promenade.

Says our reader: "As people watched him, a chap walking past wearing a Glasgow football team top did not break stride but made an exaggerated mime of putting his hand in his pocket then throwing imaginary coins in the artist's cap, and carried on walking."

ANOTHER colleague returns from his holidays and seeks me out. "My wife woke up with a massive smile on her face this morning," he almost shouts.

I wait. "I just adore the weans' felt tip pens," he added.

A READER returning from a holiday abroad says he heard the bored staff in security having a blether when one told his pal: "You missed the flight from Russia that landed today."

When the second chap asked if anything unusual had happened, the first one declared: "I asked one Russian woman to take her shoes off, and guess what? She had a smaller pair on below them ... and then another smaller pair."

Well, you have to pass the time somehow doing that job.

NEWS from Loch Lomond where Yorkshire theme park company Flamingo Land has been named preferred developer for a site at the loch beside Balloch.

It has plans for "high-quality, family-based attractions" apparently. Anyway, our favourite Loch Lomond story was of the coach full of tourists travelling past and the tour guide, microphone in hand announcing: "We are now approaching one of Scotland's most famous and most beautiful lochs ... it is called Loch Lomond."

A female American voice piped up three seats from the back and asked: "Is that where the Lock Ness Monster is?" We liked the tour guide's tactful reply of: "No madam - unless it is on holiday like yourself."

THERE are a few tourists around at this time of year. A guide at a National Trust property says he was asked by an American visitor if he had ever seen a ghost on the premises. "Never since I've been here," he replied.

But when the tourist then asked: "And how long have you been here?" he couldn't stop himself from replying: "Three hundred years."

WE have sometimes suggested that some businesses in Scotland are less than welcoming. On the other hand, Scott Barclay recounts: "On a visit to South Uist we were the sole occupants in a local hotel. The owner poured our first drinks then told us to help ourselves thereafter as his wife was in Aberdeen Maternity Hospital, and he finally had peace and quiet to watch *The Guns Of Navarone* all the way through."

JIM Nicol in Lenzie recalls his mother-in-law answering the door at the family farm in Cardross where a distressed chap told her: "I've lost my bairns." Says Jim: "She asked him, 'Goodness, when did you last see them?' Some further explanation revealed that the traveller had actually only lost his bearings, and was easily set on the right path."

OUR tales of tough landladies remind Carolyn Johnston in Paisley: "My husband, Ian, and I, on an American trip, arrived at our B&B in Tombstone, Arizona, to find no-one in the house and our room key in an envelope wedged in the unlocked front door with instructions to make ourselves at home.

"When we finally met the landlord and landlady the following day, we asked if he wasn't worried when he left the front door unlocked. He looked at us and said, 'Every house in this town has at least one gun, so nobody breaks in anywhere'."

A NEW Zealand newspaper has declared that Glasgow is one of the world's most underrated cities. As it declared: "The allegedly dangerous, ugly cousin of Edinburgh is actually amazingly friendly."

TOURISTS continued. Says James Beedie: "My wife reminded me of the time when she was on a bus tour in Stirlingshire. On board was a group of American tourists when all of a sudden there were cries from one of their group, 'Say, look at the Pyramids'. Passengers were mystified, until my wife realised they were looking at coal bings."

AN Ayrshire reader phones to tell us that the Queen is taking the King of Spain out on a trip on a glass-bottomed boat as part of his State Visit to Britain.

We can't stop ourselves from asking why, only to be told: "It's to show him the Spanish Armada."

HOLIDAY site TripAdvisor doesn't just do reviews, it's also an advice forum where a couple from Oslo asked this week: "We are going to Glasgow. We saw a programme on childhood in Scotland, and the exciting architecture of Cumbernauld came to our attention. Would it be worth going there?"

Someone merely gave them a link to a website that states: "Cumbernauld is unique in that it has a total of three 24-hour supermarkets. This is down to many of Cumbernauld's residents being afraid to come out in the daylight for fear of being mugged, and fancy their chances dodging scuzzers in the cover of darkness and when it is quieter once the off sales have all closed."

WE read that the Ayr Gaiety Theatre could face closure as the local council has cut its grant - despite pitching in quite a few quid recently to refurbish it - but that's councils for you.

We remember our erstwhile colleague Jack McLean once arguing that "Ayr Gaiety" was a contradiction as "gaiety in Ayr is a landlady giving you breakfast after half-past seven in the morning."

BIT windy in Scotland yesterday. A Paisley reader tells us he was once flying on a small Texan airline from Dallas to Charlotte in North Carolina when the stewardess announced: "The sun is shining here in Dallas but it's wet and windy in Charlotte. Why in the world y'all wanna go there I really don't know."

ONE of the new routes out of Glasgow Airport is Wizz Airlines with a three-times-a-week flight to Budapest, a Unesco World Heritage Site with the Museum of Fine Arts and Hungarian National Gallery amongst its attractions.

Clearly, the culture is a strong attraction as a Newton Mearns Diary reader tells us she was on the flight last week when a group of Glasgow lads got on board with identical T-shirts bearing the legend "Budapished!"

MUSICIAN Roy Gullane tells us: "I was talking to an exiled Glaswegian last night, down here in the Black Country, who had certainly not lost his accent. I was astonished when he told me his ageing father had herpes. He quickly corrected me with, 'Naw - a herr piece'."

OUR tales of Scottish customs officers being kind to fellow Scots reminds our old colleague Alan Hunter: "My school pal Dick Trodden, who joined HM Customs and was based at Dover, stopped a car heavily loaded, low on its springs, which to Dick's experienced eye, was obviously carrying over-the-limit supplies of booze.

"The driver was from Kelty in Fife, and assured Dick he only had his permitted limits on alcohol, claiming he was skint.

"He was waved on, with a look of absolute relief on his face, until he was told, 'Stop - I need to talk to you sir'.

"Dick, always politely spoken, launched into the West Fife patois, telling him, 'Mind and watch it when ye are gaun roond Kelty junction'."

A READER in Banchory, Aberdeenshire, noticed a hearse parked outside a gym in the town. Had someone overdone their exercising? He went over to pay his respects when he noticed the undertaker and his assistant offloading a sunbed from the hearse.

"They couldn't fit it in the vehicle they had, so we were doing them a favour," they explained. "Ye canna whack the Deeside spirit of multitasking," says our reader.

THE *Herald* archive picture of the donkeys at Ayr beach reminds

George Tomlinson: "What do the donkeys at Ayr beach get for their lunch? Half-an-hour, the same as at Blackpool.

"Aye, the old ones are the best."

OUR hearse story reminds David Will: "On a family holiday in the 1950s, on a farm in County Donegal, we used to walk to the 'one street town' of Dunkineely, where my father would treat us to an ice cream.

"On one such trip we had to clear the road for a speeding hearse, belonging to Timony's, an emporium in Donegal Town that catered for all your needs 'from the cradle to the grave'. How did we know this -from the handful of advertising flyers the driver threw from his open window as he sped past."

OUR tales of being helped by fellow Scots remind John Crawford in Lytham: "Years ago we arrived off a ferry in Newhaven in East Sussex after a fortnight driving in France. My wife had gone overboard in the hypermarkets and had stashed bottles of wine in every available bit of the car. I'd warned her we were well over the allowance and if we were caught I intended to blame it all on her.

"Of course we were stopped and the Customs Officer said, 'Hiv ye's anythin tae declare?' My wife said, 'Naw, ah'm jist knackered wi a' the travelin' and a long drive ahead o's us'. 'Well ye's had better get oan wi it' and he waved us through."

DIVIDED by a common language: a reader in the United States sends us a comment in her local newspaper which says:

"In the UK, *50 Shades of Grey* isn't a sexy book, it's the weather report."

WE are dipping our toes in Glasgow Fair stories, and retired police officer Alan Barlow in Paisley recalls: "In Rothesay in the late fifties we would meet steamers coming in for the Glasgow Fair and if we did not like the look of some of the passengers we would quietly suggest to them that they may wish to use their return tickets immediately.

"I remember seeing an old court record which noted a holidaymaker being fined for a minor crime but with the addition, 'Deported - Whence came'."

AND talking of holidays, Mungo Henning was in Montenegro where the tour guide explained that the EU had placed sanctions on Montenegro during the recent conflict with the result that the black market flourished, and cars were being stolen in Italy in order to be smuggled into Montenegro.

Says Mungo: "Once the sanctions were lifted, and a few years of normality returned, Montenegro did a large advertising campaign in Italy to boost its holiday destination status. The gist of the adverts were, 'Come and holiday in Montenegro: your car is already here'."

OUR tale of the bus driver taking the woman home to switch off her oven, reminds Andrew Foster in Cambridge, Ontario: "This corner of Ontario still has a sizeable Scottish population, and it used to extend to the polis. A good Paisley lady of our acquaintance was stopped for speeding and asked why the hurry. 'Ma shortbread's in the oven!' she told him. 'Away ye go!' and that was the end of the matter."

GORDON Rigby was sitting in a great wee pub in Rosemarkie on the Black Isle beside the fireplace where the lintel is an old marriage stone placed there in 1691, with the couple's initials I.M. and I.A. placed between the numbers so that it reads "16IMIA91". He heard a Glaswegian customer ask: "Is that the wifi code? Great that you have it in Braille."

AN Edinburgh reader says he may have spotted the laziest tourist in the city. He was walking past the Vodafone shop on Princes Street which has a huge photograph of Edinburgh Castle in its window. A young chap was positioning his girlfriend beside it so that he could take her picture "beside the castle" rather than the pair of them hiking themselves up the hill to the actual castle across the road.

And while many people visiting the capital just now are singing its praises, a warning from a visitor from Caithness who went on social media yesterday to declare: "It's £9.90 for a pint of Peroni and a bottle of Bud in Edinburgh. Madness!" Stick to Glasgow, that's what we say.

TODAY'S idle musing comes from a reader who phones to ask us: "Do you think there is someone in Nigeria just now who is telling his pal, 'I didn't get a single reply to my email so I'm just going to give all that money to charity'."

OUR esteemed sister paper the *Evening Times* yesterday referred to the weather in Glasgow as "taps aff" weather. Jim Meikle tells us he was in Copenhagen the other week where a relative who has lived there most of his life was arguing how Glasgow needed to improve its public services if it needed to introduce a hose-pipe ban after only a few days of warm weather.

This greatly puzzled Jim until further inquiry revealed that the relative had been reading about "taps aff" in Glasgow.

AS folk head off for their summer holidays, a reader in Pollokshaws muses: "Waterboarding in Guantanamo Bay sounds like great fun if you don't actually know what either of these things are."

AND at a slight tangent, George Tomlinson says: "My two friends, brothers, we're touring Donegal, and decided to visit their father's brother that neither had seen for over 20 years. They knew the village but not where he lived, so they went to the post office and asked for the directions to 'auld Mick's house' and were told that sadly Mick had died a week earlier.

"The brothers decided to offer commiserations to his wife, but when they introduced themselves, the widow said, 'He's only been dead a week and you two are over to see what you can get your hands on'."

SADLY, not many folk will realise that it is Fair Friday in Glasgow a week today. Ian McCloy in Bishopton recalls: "Many years ago my then girlfriend had arranged before she met me a holiday with her girlfriends in Spain for the Fair Fortnight.

"After the holiday one of her friends came up to me and said, 'I think it best you know that your girlfriend met a boy on the very first night and went out with him every day of the holiday. Oh and by the way, if you are thinking of dumping her, I'll go out with you'."

BEN Tourney recalled: "I was on the Waverley paddle steamer in the seventies, and just before we sailed from Ayr, a newspaper seller was sauntering along the deck, delivering in a muted intonation the message, 'Ailsa Craig washed ashore. Ailsa Craig washed ashore'. So maybe 'fake news' isn't all that new a phenomenon."

LOOKING out your summer clothes yet? As one reader tells us: "After all the holiday and winter eating I've done this year, I'm happy to report that my flip flops still fit."

WE'VE mentioned the tourists who are now appearing in Scotland as the sun begins to shine. John Rose in Fort William tells us a tourist strolled into Marshall and Pearson's ironmongers in the town and asked if they cut house keys. When the assistant said they did, she said she would like two copies, and just stood there. When the assistant asked: "Have you got the key with you?" she replied: "No. Do I need to?"

THE Nevis Range ski resort, with its cable car, will be 30 years old next year. John Rose in Fort William tells us that the company behind it ordered 3,000 pencils as souvenirs with a picture of the cable car gondola printed on them. When the order was delivered they discovered they had been sent 3,000 pencils with Venetian gondolas. Not such a good souvenir then.

THE *Herald* archive pictures of Glasgow dance halls reminded golfers at an Ayrshire club of going to the Locarno in Glasgow with one of them recalling the great line of his pal who asked a woman to dance.

Because of his youthful appearance she haughtily replied: "I don't dance with a child!" which allowed him say: "Sorry, I didn't realise you were in that condition."

OUR street vendor stories remind Patricia Watson: "Perhaps it's just a myth that in some parts of Scotland before NHS dental care, it was the practice to have every tooth removed to mark a 21st birthday, but every year on Cowal Games day in Dunoon a fruit seller used to follow the crowds and set up his stall near the park, shouting, 'Rerr juicy perrs. Nae teeth needed'."

HOW did you spend the bank holiday? A reader sadly emails: "Lie in for another hour. Move to couch. Eat snacks. Procrastinate. Wonder where day has gone. Sigh."

JOHN Dunlop recalls when he and his pal were bingo callers at Butlins in Ayr in the seventies. Says John: "We were told, time without number, to 'rummle yir ba's son' - sometimes with due cause. Still recovering from the previous night's intake at the Pig and Whistle or the Stuart Ballroom, we would sometimes run through games, which started at nine in the morning, just making it up without using any balls at all. Even repeating numbers. And still they came back for more. Happy days."

WE don't know if it's an Edinburgh thing, but Tom Strang was looking at the Royal Mile Luxury Rooms on the hotel website booking.com and read that facilities included "linen, TV, toilet paper".

Is it only in Edinburgh that they would brag about supplying it?

DOWN memory lane alert. Dougie McNicol recalls, after our story about open windows, of the radio show *Round the Horne*. "Horne had a rich, BBC announcer-type voice and a dead-pan delivery. He announced, 'In the current warm weather, many of you will have your windows open and if your radio is too loud, it may annoy your neighbours. Another good way to annoy them is to set fire to their dustbins'."

NICE weather for May. A reader sums up many a conversation at this time: "It's nice out...but not quite warm enough to sit outside."

Temperature rises by one degree.

"No, too hot."

THE company Freeflush has analysed British weather statistics and has claimed that Glasgow is the coldest and wettest city in the UK. It reminds us of the tourist in Glasgow, making conversation with a taxi driver, asking, 'Does it always rain here?' The driver replied, 'Naw', then added after a significant pause, 'Sometimes it snaws'."

MUCH discussion about *The Herald* archive picture of the school cruise ships that went to Spain and Portugal in the sixties. Says Paul O'Sullivan: "Some pupils from my school went on the Portugal cruise in the summer of 1967. When they were being shown round the football stadium in Lisbon, they pulled out knives and plastic bags to take away bits of the turf where Celtic had won the European Cup a couple of months earlier."

THE Herald archive picture of the Scottish schoolchildren on the school cruise to Portugal and Spain on the SS *Dunera* reminds a reader: "We were on the trip from a girls' school in Bothwell. When we got to Lisbon some boys started following us, so the nuns from the school marched us straight back to the ship and we saw nothing of Lisbon."

A READER notices the advertisement in *The Herald* for The Spirit Of Skye Festival later this month and reads that the programme includes: "Whisky distillers, award-winning brewers, gin crafters and axe throwing." Says our reader: "So nothing to worry about there then."

WE asked for your Fair Fortnight stories ahead of Fair Friday, and a Kelvinside reader recalls being at the Bobby Jones dance hall in Ayr many moons ago in his youth, when a young Glasgow girl on holiday during the Fair was being enthusiastically "winched" at the side of a hall by a fellow holidaymaker.

The girl drew herself away from the clinch to tell the chap: "If yer lookin' fur ma tonsils, they were removed when I was eight."

17

Trains and Boats and Planes

Travelling is a great way to have brief contact with strangers, often with amusing results.

DONALD Grant, in Paisley, tells us: "Was just on the bus on a very wet morning. A well-dressed elderly lady came on, sat down, and made a couple of small wipes on the steamed-up window. Seated behind her was a woman and a wee boy of around five years of age, who piped up, 'Granny, is that the Queen waving to people?'"

WE have to agree with Craig Deeley who makes the observation: "There's no way of closing a window on the bus without appearing grumpy."

HAPPY birthday to the Glasgow Subway, 120 years old yesterday. I still remember writer Cliff Hanley telling a BBC reporter from London the Subway was unique in that if you fell asleep you still ended up where you wanted to go.

And any excuse to mention Chic Murray, who asked at Hillhead ticket office: "Does the next train have a buffet car?" When the puzzled worker said no, he replied: "I'll just wait for the next one then."

THE 120th anniversary of the Glasgow Subway reminds Bill Mitchell: "As a student in the seventies I used the 'shoogly' every day. The late-night trains had a conductor who, summer and winter, wore an ankle-length overcoat with his whistle attached to a chain that reached the floor. He would wander up and down the carriage helping himself to chips from passengers' carry-out suppers, so presumably offsetting his wages by never having to eat at home."

OUR mention of the Glasgow Subway's 120th birthday reminds a reader of the driver announcing over the Tannoy at Hillhead station to a packed train: "Could passengers please move up the carriage?" When no one moved this was followed by an even more deadpan announcement: "Could passengers please assist the passengers who are deaf to move up the carriage?"

GOING further back, older readers still talk wistfully of the Subway smell before it was modernised. We always thought the best description was given by reader William Haddow, who described it as: "Warm and slightly stale, a sweet and musty mixture of fag and pipe smoke, vinegar in newsprint chip-pokes, damp and decaying brickwork, Brylcreem, and Alberto VO5, all cut through with the acrid electric smell of hot insulation and burnt carbon." Now that's nostalgia.

THE Diary story about TV quiz show *University Challenge* reminds Jim Morrison: "Sitting at our evening meal on a Sealink ferry in Larne, Northern Ireland, in the eighties, we were surprised when Donald, our third engineer, answered question after question correctly when *University Challenge* came on BBC Northern Ireland. "Donald, your knowledge is amazing," I told him. "No really," said Donald. "I watched it on BBC Scotland when I was hame last night."

A READER emails to say: "Trick people into doing an impression of someone with a wasp in their clothes by shouting 'Tickets please!' on a busy train."

TAXI tales continued. Says David Martin: "I remember getting into a taxi with John, a fellow teacher. The taxi driver, hearing our conversation, piped up, 'Are you two teachers, then? I could never be a teacher'. To which John said, 'You should have stuck in at school then'.
 "The driver was less anxious to converse after that."

JOHN Park in Lanarkshire tells us about a local teenager finishing school and taking a year off before going to university. He decided to take a temporary job with ScotRail in order to get some cash. Friends immediately dubbed it his "mind-the-gap year".

NEXT month sees the 50th anniversary of the opening of the Aviemore Centre tourist attraction. Dugald MacAngus, the then catering manager, tells us they ran out of ice to chill the champagne bottles at the opening, but it was so cold the water fountains in the square had frozen over so they took pick-axes to the fountains and filled several dustbins with ice and put the champagne in the bins.

WE asked for your Aviemore stories to mark the 50th anniversary of the Aviemore Centre and Jean Jardine in Barrhead recalls her mum and dad, plus herself, her 6ft 2ins brother, and the family spaniel, squeezing themselves into a borrowed Mini Cooper 50 years ago to drive to her granny's in Banffshire.

"When we got to Aviemore we needed petrol but the petrol station was shut for the evening. We had no food other than a sweetie machine which dispensed Polo mints. I tried to sleep with the dog on my lap and my brother's knees digging into the seat. "Next morning we got our petrol and drove off - to find a 24-hour petrol station round the next bend."

AN Uddingston reader tells us he knew his wife was a nervous flyer but he thought she hit a new low when they were returning from an autumn break in Spain and a baby behind them started crying. His wife looked anxiously round then whispered to him: "Wait, why is he screaming? What does he know that we don't?"

A RUTHERGLEN reader was on the train from London when he watched a woman leave her newspaper with a half-finished crossword on the table. The chap sitting opposite couldn't resist it, picked up the paper and started filling in the blanks.

He was very embarrassed when the woman returned as she had actually just gone to the loo and had not left the train at the previous station, and then looked around to finish her crossword.

A WHITECRAIGS reader tells us a woman got on the train into Glasgow yesterday, began rubbing at her coat, and told her pal: "Every coat is a fur coat when your cat sleeps on it."

THE news story about the pilot being jailed for being drunk reminds us of the reader on a trip to London and buying some coloured sugar he had promised for his wife. He asked the assistant to bubble-wrap it as he thought he had better put it in his suitcase rather than risk it in his hand luggage. As he told the assistant: "I don't know why I am asking you to wrap this - how could I use a bag of sugar as a weapon on a plane?" "The pilot might be diabetic, sir" replied the assistant.

TODAY'S piece of whimsy comes from a Dennistoun reader who phones to tell us: "At this time of year you always get folk complaining about crying babies on airplanes. But I always tell them, 'Better than a crying pilot'."

THE Ministry of Defence says that the next destroyer to be built at Govan will be named HMS *Glasgow*. We recall the previous HMS *Glasgow* being used for a photo-call in the early nineties when the MoD announced that Wrens would be able to serve at sea and a number of Wrens were interviewed on board *Glasgow*.

One of the Wrens, from Hamilton, came out with the memorable line: "Lots of wives are really terrified we are going to run off with their husbands.

"If a husband is going to be unfaithful to his wife, he doesn't have to go to sea to do it."

THE Glasgow Subway is still the place where strangers will chat. John Mulholland was speaking to a chap from Manchester who told him he had been on the Subway in order to attend his daughter's graduation at Glasgow University. He was sitting there, smartly dressed for the occasion, when the auld fella opposite leaned over and asked knowingly: "Graduation ceremony?" "Yes," replied the puzzled chap, who then asked: "How did you know?" "Because nobody ever travels on the Subway wi' shoes as shiny as that," came the reply.

TODAY'S piece of silliness comes from Gary Delaney, who says: "I'm not saying this ferry is cheap, but the gym on the bottom deck is just two rows of oars."

WE can feel his pain. Author Ian Spring, in his book *Real Glasgow* in which he tours the city, writes about taking the Subway to Partick from town but nods off, and comes to at Govan.

Says Ian: "Govan is one of the larger stations and has an entrance either end of each platform. As the train pulled into the station I noted a train pulling into the opposite platform. I jumped off, ran up and down the stairs and just caught the closing doors of the train.

"Looking round I realised I had run down the wrong stairs and got back on the same train."

THE *Herald's* archive picture of Glasgow's first driver-only bus reminds John Bannerman in Kilmaurs, Ayrshire, of the friendly, family-run bus that took folk from the village to Kilmarnock for shopping. Says John: "After I got on one day, a few stops later, Wee Bella jumped up and said, 'Stoap the bus, Jock - ah'll need tae go back hame, ah've left the mince oan the gas!' "The driver asked if anybody was in a hurry, and when everyone replied 'No!' he took Bella back to her house and waited for her to turn the gas off."

TODAY sees the launch, as it were, of the film *Dunkirk* when the British Expeditionary Force was saved from France. What is perhaps not known is that the paddle steamer *Waverley*, the precursor to the present one which replaced her, was among the flotilla of boats.

Then Captain John Cameron later revealed when they arrived "a great cheer went up and one lad shouted, 'Haw Wullie, we're oan the auld *Waverley* goin' to Rothesay. We're awright noo'." Sadly the *Waverley* was sunk - but many men were saved as its wooden seats floated to the surface with the troops clinging to them.

A READER hears a fellow member of his Ayrshire golf club comment: "The people who make car commercials grossly over-estimate the amount of time I spend driving around in a desert."

TIME to flush our toilet stories, as Jim Currie recalls: "Subma-riner Alistair Mars once told of submarine commanders visiting the mother ship, where the ship's captain explained it had under-gone a refurbishment and he would not tolerate any graffiti in the newly painted toilets. He did concede though it would be hard to better the previous graffiti when someone had written, 'This bloody house is no use at all, the seat's too high and the hole's too small'. "Below in a different hand was, 'To which I must add the obvious retort, your bum's too big and your legs too short'."

TERRIBLE delays for British Airways passengers at the week-end. It reminds Ian Craig of waiting at Edinburgh Airport for a flight where fellow passengers began reminiscing about the days of flying when there was a smoking and non-smoking section on the plane. Ian admits he did laugh when one of them opined: "That's a bit like having a peeing section in a swimming pool."

THE news that the missing piece of the M8 between Baillieston and Newhouse will open later this month reminds us of the old gag of the elderly lady being stopped on the M8 by police for driving very slowly. She told them that she thought the M8 signs meant she had to drive at eight miles an hour.

Before leaving, the traffic cops asked the ill-looking old gentleman next to her if he was ok and he replied that they had just come off the M90.

SIMPLE pleasures. A Hyndland reader tells us that when she sees some huge car with tinted windows obscuring the driver she simply waves at them in the hope that they worry about the tint wearing off.

SUNSHINE in Glasgow yesterday. John Mulholland heard a chap in the pub declare: "My wife announced that she fancied going for a drive with the top off. That worried me - we don't have a convertible."

OUR tales of pipe bands remind Gordon Casely of being a member of the Glasgow Transport Pipe Band which was playing on an open-top bus in Manchester in a procession of transport through the ages. Says Gordon: "We drove the 16-mile route at eight miles an hour. The pipe-major ordered the set 'Scotland The Brave' and 'Rowan Tree', and we played those never-endingly throughout an interminable two hours.

"The pipey explained later, 'We were passing at eight miles an hour, so no-one would hear us repeat them'."

A WHITECRAIGS reader passes on that he was on the train into Glasgow yesterday when a young girl got on and told her pals she met: "My hair's so amazing today I hope I bump into all my ex-boyfriends."

A COLLEAGUE spots I'd not been in the office for a few days and feels the need to saunter over and tell me: "Recreate the feeling of being in a multi-storey car park by driving around in circles with a piece of paper in your mouth."

18

Ripped Jeans, Old Houses & Lost Gloves

Some stories defy categorisation. They are just daft or funny.

DAFT story of the day comes from a reader in Aberdeen, who emails: "I went back to my home town and decided to visit the house I grew up in.

"I went up and knocked on the door and asked the folk who live there if I could go inside and see my old room. They said no.

"I have to tell you, my parents can be really mean at times."

NOTICED teenage girls' fashion trends these days? A Glasgow girl told her friends last week: "My cousin took her washing up to my gran's for her to do. When she went back to pick it up, gran had sewn her ripped jeans up. I'm crying with laughter."

TODAY'S piece of daftness comes from Neil who says: "It's proper chilly today - even my gate post is wearing a glove."

OUR old chum George Wilkie gets all nostalgic and tells us: "Helping us with rationing after the war, our relatives in Canada would send food parcels. We were inducted into the mysteries of tinned Campbell soups and fruit puddings. They all seemed to expand in water ... just short of miraculous.

"Near Christmas the parcel arrived, my mother decided that one of the powdered packages was soup. Mixed with boiling water it was dreadful and was promptly poured down the sink. A letter then arrived bearing the sad news that our uncle had died. "His widow had put his ashes in the parcel and could we scatter them near the Forth Bridge?"

A READER combines his love of films with frustration at a daily nuisance at home by telling us: "You had me at hello. You lost me at have you been in an accident that wasn't your fault?"

ON at the weekend was the return of TV karaoke programme *The X Factor* which is not, it has to be said, everybody's cup of tea.

A reader heard a young chap in the pub last night tell a young woman, "Me and the pals played the *X Factor* drinking competition last night."

"Oh how do you play that?" she asked.

"Every time it comes on the telly we turn it off and go to the pub," he replied.

A MILNGAVIE reader emails us with the suggestion: "I think an enterprising youngster could make a bob or two by going round the houses offering to fill in all those adult colouring-in books we've bought but never got round to using."

AN Edinburgh reader tells us he was invited to a friend's surprise birthday party by the chap's wife who had everyone sworn to secrecy about the big night. He tells us that his pal made a speech where he declared that his enjoyment of the night was slightly spoiled by the knowledge that all his family and friends can easily lie to his face without him knowing.

TODAY'S piece of daftness comes from Moose Allain who passes on the telephone conversation - "Who's calling please?" "Mr Whitcombe with a b". "And the bee's name?"

DEBBIE Fleming in Canada remarks: "I called an old school friend and asked what he was doing. He replied that he was working on 'aqua-thermal treatment of ceramics, aluminium and steel under a constrained environment'. I was impressed.

"But on further enquiring I learnt that he was washing dishes, under his wife's supervision."

TODAY'S piece of daftness comes from a Bishopbriggs reader who emails: "I was hooked on auctions after only going once... going twice."

I TRY to look busy, but a colleague still feels the need to come over and interrupt me. When I finally ask him what's happening, he tells me: "The wife has left me because I told her she was a rubbish pilot. I can't believe she took off like that."

TODAY'S piece of whimsy comes from Mike Ginn, who says: "Most bags of sand live a tough life stopping floods.

"But some, the lucky ones, live a leisurely life tied to the basket of a hot air balloon."

A READER in Glasgow heard the woman at the next table to him in a coffee shop tell her pals: "The next time someone tells me to expect the unexpected, I'm going to slap them on the face, and ask them if they expected that."

OUR occasional foray into wedding speeches reminds a Killearn reader: "The best man in his wedding speech said that 20 years ago the mother of the bride had sent her to bed with a dummy, and tonight history would be repeating itself."

A BEARSDEN reader writes to us: "I just put on a jacket I had not worn for a while. I found three £1 coins in a pocket. I could have purchased Rangers FC, Prestwick Airport and British Home Stores."

FOR sheer daftness, a reader in Kelvinbridge phoned to tell us: "I just read a book about the Stockholm Syndrome. It wasn't that good at first, but by the end I really liked it."

NICE sunny day in Glasgow yesterday but not as warm as the south of England. As Gordon Johnstone down south remarked: "They should turn all them stupid wind farms on to full power to cool us down."

A READER in Hillhead sends us this confession: "I find it embarrassing that 90 per cent of my searches on Google are just common words that I wasn't sure how to spell.

"And yes, I Googled 'embarrassing'."

NOT had a wedding story for a while. Matt Vallance tells us: "A wedding photographer's wife was telling me her job was to have the subjects of the next picture lined up, ready to go.

This worked fine until she spent 15 fruitless minutes trying to find 'Mary Dawn'.

"The bride, apparently, had wanted a picture of those who were 'mairried-oan' to her immediate family."

19
Celebration Time

Christmas, New Year, whatever the occasion, we Scots love to make the most of a festival or party.

A GLASGOW reader was picking his daughter up from a party in the West End, which made him reminisce about going to his first party there a generation before. He recalled: "The music was a bit loud, and the neighbour through the wall started knocking on it.

"I still remember a drunk staring at the wall and shouting, 'There's not a door there! You'll have to come round'."

SOME folk were popping into their offices for a couple of days between Christmas and New Year. A reader in Glasgow heard a workmate explain about his Christmas presents: "So basically my family must think I smell, drink to excess, and have threadbare socks."

FUNNY how healthy eating is quietly forgotten at this time of year. As Peter Smith reflected: "As a personal tribute to David Bowie, I've made a whole tin of Heroes last just for one day."

A YOUNGER reader passes on a conversation he heard in a Glasgow club post-Christmas when a young girl dressed to the nines told her pal: "That guy over there is getting on ma nerves."

When her friend looked over then told her: "He's no even lookin' at you," she replied: "That's why he's gettin' oan ma nerves."

SADLY, we cannot track down the Glasgow church where we are told that, at the Christmas service, the minister was explaining to the Sunday school members about the three kings bringing presents to the Baby Jesus and how he asked them: "There is a higher authority than kings. Do we know who that is, children?"

A tentative voice came back with: "Aces?"

A READER out shopping in Newton Mearns yesterday tells us he bumped into an old pal and asked him what he got for Christmas. "Did you see the new BMW at the front of the car park?"

replied his pal. When our reader went "Wow!" his pal continued: "Well I got a tie just the same colour."

THERE were of course the occasional harsh words spoken at the Christmas meal. A photographer friend confesses to us that he gets a little aggrieved when people put his pictures down to his camera equipment.

He was at his girlfriend's mother's for Christmas where she said: "Lovely pictures. You must have a very good camera." His reply of: "Lovely dinner. You must have very good pots and pans," didn't seem to go down too well.

JEAN Murphy says her grandchildren, aged twelve and nine, probably had a good idea in advance of what they got on Christmas morning.

"They no longer look in cupboards or under beds for Christmas presents," she says.

"They check their parents' online order histories. Things ain't what they used to be."

GETTING old continued. Says Bruce Skivington: "Going into the supermarket the other day I pointed out a sign saying 'Only eight sleeps to Christmas' to my wife. She replied, 'In your case that's 16 if you include your afternoon nap'."

CHRISTMAS presents are being bought and a Glasgow father tells us: "This is when the kids discuss what to get me for Christmas.

One of them insists on a shirt, the other suggests socks.

"So the argument always ends in a tie."

AND a Bearsden reader who helped his wife wrap the Christmas presents says: "No matter how old I get if you give me an empty Christmas wrapping-paper tube I'm going to hit someone on the head with it."

KATE Woods gets us in the Christmas spirit by recounting: "Last December my cousin was a few Christmas cards short, and asked her daughter to get some. Local shops were sold out and eventually she went into a corner shop with the permanent grill over the window in a less salubrious area. On asking the pleasant shopkeeper if he had any cards left he reached for a box, then said, 'Aye hen, but the only ones left are the s*** wans'."

AS the office nights out get under way, a Glasgow chap in a city centre pub at the weekend tells us he was chatting to a toper wearing a paper hat who nodded at a raucous table and explained:

"We've reached the point where I have to decide whether to stop my drunk mate from making a fool of himself, or to film it on my phone and put it on YouTube."

RHYS James speaks for many who have been given Advent calendars when he declares: "Right well, there's literally not a '4' on here. I'm looking and there's not one. What idiot makes an advent calendar with no... oh, it's there."

DECEMBER now, so the pubs will soon be full of amateur drinkers on their nights out. A Glasgow reader recalls being in the pub last December when a chap heard a foreign accent at the bar and asked the young woman: "Where are you from?" She replied: "The United States."

He kept going with: "Which part?" And she replied: "All of me."

WE foolishly asked a colleague if he had done his Christmas shopping. "My son said he wanted an Action Man for Christmas but now he tells me he wants a Red Indian. I've been trying to put a brave face on it."

HALLOWE'EN soon, and a reader working out his costume tells us: "The great thing about dressing up as Donald Trump is that no matter how fake your wig is, you will still look like Donald Trump."

VALENTINE'S Day today - well we did warn you - and a reader reminds us of the loudmouth in the Glasgow bar who announced: "The wife said she wanted to be pampered on Valentine's Day.

"But I had a look at them in the supermarket, and there's no way she would fit in them."

AND a Glasgow reader sums up today for many with the poem: Roses are red, Violets are blue, They had neither at the garage, So it's De-Icer for you.

BURNS Night this week so well done to Police Scotland for posting on social media that there was a report of a public disorder incident at Alloway Auld Kirk where Ayr resident Mr Thomas o' Shanter claimed to have seen women in a state of undress cavorting in the ruins.

Added Police Scotland: "Safer Communities officer PC Jamie Dunlop stated, 'This incident highlights the dangers of consuming too much alcohol and travelling home unaccompanied. We encourage anyone going out and attending licensed premises to plan their night and ensure that they have arranged transport home. Avoid joining groups of unknown persons as they may not have the same idea of a good night out as you'."

MORE signs you are getting old, as Ron Fretwell in East Kilbride tells us he was at a splendid Burns Breakfast at the local old folks club where it was decided to have a breakfast and not a supper, as many of the oldsters don't like going out in the evening.

A GUEST arrived at a Burns Supper on Glasgow's Southside at the weekend with her baby wearing a kilt. As the gathered women oohed and aahed at the child someone asked where on earth you could possibly buy such a small kilt.

"The Build-A-Bear Workshop" she confided.

WE weren't going to mention Valentine's Day again, but we should make space for that cheeky Tory MSP Murdo Fraser who wound up Nats yesterday with the poem: "Roses are red, Violets are blue, If there's a second Indyref, You'll lose that too."

AS the Burns Nights get into full swing, a piper of the Diary's acquaintance tells us: "So far my January could be summed up as 'Four Haggises and a Funeral'."

IT was the first day back at work yesterday for some workers after Christmas and New Year, and one reader in Glasgow confesses that he wished his office Christmas party had not actually been held in the office. It was only when he returned yesterday that he recalled he ended the drink-fuelled evening hiding in the supplies cupboard. When he heard someone passing he would jump out shouting "Supplies!"

AS the Burns Suppers begin to wind down for another year, Brian Donohoe in Ayrshire tells us: "Was at a Burns Supper at the weekend sitting at a table with singer Sydney Devine. I asked him if he still gets knickers thrown at him when he performs. 'I do, but they're getting much bigger nowadays', he replied."

SO how was your New Year? As Trisha Martin tells us: "A respectable widow was returning to her house on Arran around 00.45am on January 1, having given a guest a lift home. Two men were leaning over next door's wall. 'Sorry, hen', says one.

""That's ok', she says. 'Happy New Year'. And the chap replied, 'I'd offer tae shake yer haun but I've just had a pee. But I could gie you a kiss'.

"The widow regretfully declined!"

SOMETIMES Glasgow really does live up to the stereotype. One of four brightly-painted temporary Santa statues in Sauchiehall Street was removed and placed in The Garage nightclub for safekeeping after it was damaged - somebody had punched it.

A spokesman for The Garage commented philosophically: "Obviously the person who punched Santa had not had a good Christmas themselves."

FOLK will be heading back to work this week after the Christmas and New Year break. We remember the Glasgow City Council worker we met at this time last year in Gregg's who told us: "I always take a dozen doughnuts in to my colleagues on the first day back. To see the looks of torment on the faces of the ones who have started a New Year diet is worth every penny."

HAPPY New Year of course. A reader swears to us he was in Ashton Lane after the bells and a hirsute chap turned to his mates and asked: "So guys, are we still doing the beard thing in 2017 or can we put that behind us?"

A BEARSDEN reader emails with the question: "Can you imagine the first person to sing 'Happy Birthday', standing there belting it out, no one joining in as they didn't know what he was on about?"

ORANGE Walks are bringing a bit of colour to our streets just now. An Ayrshire reader tells us: "I was driving into Kilwinning on Saturday night when I had to swerve to avoid a gentleman who clearly thought wearing an orange collarette gave him carte blanche to walk down the middle of the road at any time, not only when following a flute band."

AN AYRSHIRE golfer tells us he asked a fellow player at his club how he had enjoyed a wedding he had been invited to. He replied: "You don't fully know your own strength until someone tries to pull you on to a dance floor against your will."

20
Competition

Our Christmas competition was to take one letter out of a film title and make an even more interesting film. Suggestions included:

Pint Break: Glasgow surfer takes a week off the bevvy (Chris Kerr).

Bob & Carol & Ted & Lice: ménage à trois discover the pitfalls of being naughty (Billy McKnight).

The Fat And The Furious: Boxing Day sales begin in Glasgow (Peter Mohan).

Now White: What Trump voters hope America will be when the wall is built (Nan Spowart).

The Magnificent Seve: film about the great golfer.

It's A Wonderful Lie: Brexit.

One of Our Pies Is Missing: Kilmarnock FC find themselves one delicacy short (Danny McDonald).

There's Something About May: Cameron Diaz plays the girl who surprises everyone by becoming Prime Minister (David Donaldson).

The Greatest How On Earth: the world still can't come to terms with Donald Trump as president-elect (Hugh Clark).

An Inconvenient Ruth: biopic of Scottish politician who challenges party orthodoxy (Harry Clark).

Life of Bran: he's not the Messiah. He's a veggie naughty boy (David Walker).

All Quiet on the Western Font: at last an uninterrupted christening in Kelvinside (Duncan Mcintyre).

The Pelican Brie: Julia Roberts and Denzel Washington chase a big-beaked bird who has stolen his cheese (Ian Elston).

Coo Running: Scotland's answer to the Spanish tradition (Carl Williamson).

Petty Woman: row over how much Theresa May paid for leather trousers (Graeme Stewart).

Love Is A Many Splendored Hing: Romeo and Juliet, tenement style (Catherine Woods).

The Pink Panter: an attempt at the 10K on an unseasonably hot day (Gordon Cubie).

Indiana Jones and the Temple of Doo: intrepid archaeologist stumbles on a strange cult of bird-worshippers in darkest Lanarkshire (Ken Johnson).

The Bird: the chilling story of a psychotic Glaswegian fiancée (Robert A. Livingstone).

The Remains of the Da: cannibalism in a Coatbridge family (John Samson).

All Quit on the Western Front: the order comes through for everyone to retreat (Hugh Clark).

A River Runs Through T: documentary about a typical day at T in the Park.

Jurassic Par: Jim Jefferies comes out of retirement as Dunfermline Athletic's injury crisis deepens (Frank Bendoris).

The Best Ears of Our Lives: Mr Spock Tribute Movie (Bill Jamieson).

Whisk Galore: set in a new kitchen equipment shop (George Crawford).

Het: Pacino and DeNiro go head-to-head in testosterone-fuelled game of tig.

Far From the Adding Crowd: accountant looks forward to the festive break (Bobby Dunn).

Oldeneye: James Bond visits the opticians as he can't see his enemies clearly (Frances Woodward).

Brie Encounter: stoic, ill-fated romance starts with a chance meeting at the Waitrose cheese counter (John Harkin).

Hello Doll: a musical set in Maryhill (Roy Crichton).

Forrest Gum: life in a rubber plantation (Tom Fleming).

Pretty Oman: Arabian state tarts itself up (John Mulholland).

Dead Pets Society: canine zombies conspire against humans (David Hamilton).

Chariots of Fir: an epic road movie about the rugged truckers who bring Christmas trees to the cities (Alison Campbell).

The Killin of Sister George: a nurse's reflection of growing up in rural Scotland (Allan Langley).

Lady And The Tram: a Morningside matron's attempt to get the line extended to her doorstep (Nan Spowart).

Doctor Hivago: patient's advice to GP unsure of what he should prescribe (Ian Barnett).

Hadowlands: Sir Anthony Hopkins remembers his visits to a bygone Glasgow off-sales (Bill Cassidy).

A Face In The Crow: Day in the life of a regular at a Bishopbriggs tavern (James Robertson).

A Sot in the Dark: a drunk Inspector Clouseau remains clueless (Martin Laing).

Close Encounters of the Hird Kind: an evening with Dame Thora (Scott Macintosh).

Goodbye Mr Hips: orthopaedic staff wave farewell to another successful replacement patient (James Robertson).

The Jungle Boo: Celtic fans express anger as team lose a game at Parkhead (Ian Mouat).

Robin Hod: weepy tale of a labourer who steals bricks to build houses for the poor (Cameron Bell).

Twelve Years a Slav: biopic about Melania Trump's battle to get an American passport (Robert Menzies).

Ocky: Sylvester Stallone takes up darts (Malcolm Campbell).

Whit Christmas: A Glaswegian struggles to remember the festive period (Brian Logan).

The Parent Tap: the bank of mum and dad (Harry Shaw).

Star Was: the life story of this year's X Factor winner (John Dunlop).

Particus: slave revolt in Glasgow's West End (Alan Barlow).

Mutiny on the Bunty: editorial differences split staff on girls' comic (David Will).

Pint Blank: two friends try to recall the events of the previous night in the pub (Ian Anderson).

Aint Your Wagon: dispute over vehicle ownership (Mike Ritchie).

Gentlemen Refer Blondes: an upmarket dating agency (Gerry Minnery).

Whisk Galore: starring Mary Berry (Isabel McLeod).

Bogie Nights: the story of Cinderella's wee pal Sneezy with a cold (Andy Cameron).

One With the Wind: my dog! (Mary Duncan).

Gone With The Win: Clydebank syndicate ticket holder does a runner.

21

Not Forgotten

Fond memories of those no longer with us.

SAD to hear of the death of actor Freddie Boardley, who was a kenspeckle face in Glasgow's west end. We liked the subtle dig from *Rab C. Nesbitt* writer Ian Pattison who had Freddie appearing three times in *Rab C.* - first as a council assistant, then as Lord Provost, and finally as a gangster. "He became more respectable each time," said Ian.

THE great golfer Arnold Palmer has passed away. As our old colleague Alistair Nicol recalled: "I met him at a dinner at Royal Troon in the 1980s prior to The Open. He revealed that as a previous winner of The Open at Troon he had been made an honorary member of the club. He was then sent a demand for a £650 levy to put the new roof on the clubhouse. Being a much classier dude than those running the club, he sent them a cheque."

AND we also recall Arnold's tenuous connection to the take-over of Glasgow Rangers. Former Rangers director Alastair Johnston met current owner Dave King at a golf tournament in Hawaii when King, already a successful businessman, had volunteered to caddy for Arnold Palmer, a boyhood hero. Alastair phoned then owner David Murray and told him: "I'm in Hawaii with a caddy from Castlemilk who wants to put millions into the club."

Murray replied: "Have you been up all night drinking Mai Tais?"

THE *Herald* obituary of former Scotland and Hawick rugby player Billy Hunter reminds Hugh Brennan: "After over 20 years of turning out for the Greens, Billy had had enough and decided to retire. His team mates were congratulating him and saying how much they would miss him as well as going over games they had played, battles they had all gone through on the field, and wondering what were they all going to do without him in the side.

"When they had just about finished, from the corner of the dressing room George Stevenson, his former international colleague asked, 'Fit 'ill ye be daein' wi' yer auld bits?'"

WE always liked the style of *Star Wars* actress Carrie Fisher.

When she went on a luxury train vacation in Scotland on the *Royal Scotsman* with her French bulldog Gary last year, she simply handed a note to staff stating that Gary needed a meal of hamburgers and fat-free bacon followed by vanilla ice-cream.

Most of us are lucky to get a Kit-Kat on a train.

TALKING of bad news about celebrities, a reader heard a fellow toper in a Glasgow bar yesterday declare: "Remember when some folk described themselves as 'doctor to the stars'? You don't hear them bragging about that these days."

SAD to hear of the death of Raymond Jacobs, *The Herald's* former golf correspondent, and a true gentleman. He once told the story of covering a European Amateur Team Championship in The Hague where an enthusiastic volunteer operated the telex machine that sent the reporters' copy.

Raymond suggested he and the others express their appreciation of her work with a bouquet of flowers. "That would not be appropriate," a Dutch official frowned. "Why?" asked Raymond. "Because she is a member of our royal family."

YES it's been some year, 2016, but as singer James Blunt told followers on social media: "If you thought 2016 was bad - I'm releasing an album in 2017."

OUR mention of the late Raymond Jacobs, *The Herald's* golf correspondent, having a colourful turn of phrase reminds a fellow journalist of playing on *The Herald's* golf outing at a very posh

East Lothian course. His group was teeing off at the third when the club secretary shouted over at them to hurry up as they were delaying some members. The actual members were still on the first hole.

Raymond later wrote to the club captain, thanking him for a great day on a great course with superb dining. He then added the observation that the captain should perhaps suggest to the club secretary "that he should stop acting like a boating pond attendant".

SAD to hear of the death of former East Renfrewshire Tory MP Allan Stewart, he of the mutton-chop whiskers. A colleague once went to interview him at his home near Neilston, where the garden was full of stone hedgehogs. Allan himself was wearing a hedgehog tie and revealed he was a member of the British Hedge-hog Preservation Society.

He joked that hedgehogs had never changed over the thousands of years they had been on earth - much like the Tory Party.

ACTOR Peter Vaughan, who played the sinister prisoner Grouty in Ronnie Barker's *Porridge*, has died.

A little-known fact is that he attended Celtic's European Cup final against Feyenoord in Milan in 1970. A Celtic fan once wrote on a fans' messageboard: "In the San Siro we were sitting beside three Dutch supporters who kept letting off they horrible aerosol klaxon horns. My Da was beelin'. Then Peter Vaughan sat beside us wearing a beige mohair coat and, believe it or not, a Celtic scarf. The three Dutchmen pressed the klaxons again, and he stood up, (huge man by the way) and said in his gangster-type voice, 'Do that again and you'll be blowing them out your backsides'."

THE death of former Cuban leader Fidel Castro reminds us of when Labour politician Brian Wilson brought a bottle of Cuban whisky back from the Caribbean and *The Herald* took it into a Glasgow bar for locals to do a tasting and say what they thought of it. "Should be renamed Castro GTX," was by far the best response.

SAD to hear of the death of radio presenter Sir Jimmy Young, who was far more astute than some folk realise. Years ago in a *Herald* interview, he was asked about the most stupid thing he had done, and thrice-married Jimmy replied: "Marrying my second wife. We were having an affair, and she told me that didn't mean I had to marry her. However, when I was young my father told me, 'If a woman is good enough to sleep with, she is good enough to marry'. Dad's advice was pretty stupid. I should have taken hers."

FORMER Kilmarnock MP Willie McKelvey, one of life's decent people, has died. Willie was such a man of the people, he even owned greyhounds. He once gave a *Herald* sports writer a tip on the horses but added: "Just to warn you - my tips have put more folk in the grubber than the Thatcher Government."
Being an Ayrshire MP he was influenced by The Bard, and

when the boring subject of subsidiarity came up at Westminster, Willie told the Scottish Secretary: "Will he relate with clarity, to Charity McGarrity from Inverarity, that she will not have subsidiarity, but that she, like the rest of Scotland, will have to remain in the mode of subserviarity?" Sadly Ian Lang was not able to rhyme his dull answer.

CORONATION Street fans are mourning the death of actress Jean Alexander who played downtrodden Hilda Ogden.

We always liked Jean's description of the character she played when she once remarked: "I liked playing her - but I wouldn't want her living next door to me."

THE Herald's obituary of boxing manager Lou Duva reminds reader Bill Rutherford in Galashiels: "There once was a quote from Lou, which could only come from a boxing promoter, when he said, 'Every five or 10 years along comes the fight of the century'."

Sounds like something a member of the SNP might say.

MIXED views on Irish politician Martin McGuinness who died yesterday. We just recall when he moved into government as education minister he visited a Belfast primary school where one of the little ones said he was keen on fishing.

Martin, in best politician manner, asked the lad what he used for bait. To the delight of the grown-ups standing around, the young chap piped up: "We just bate them over the head with a big stick."

THE death of rock 'n' roll legend Chuck Berry is sad, but he was not always the easiest person to get on with, it has to be said. Scots-born photographer Albert Watson once said in an interview that Chuck was the most difficult person he had worked with - and that he had walked out after only four pictures were taken.

Shortly afterwards Albert received a DVD of a film Keith Richards of the Rolling Stones had made with Chuck, and Keith had written a note with it stating: "You're not the only one. He put me through hell."

SADDENED by the death of Lisbon Lion Tommy Gemmell.

We always liked Tommy's reply when he was ever asked what it was like to score in a European Cup Final. "Which one son?" he would say as he did indeed score in two finals.

Our sports colleagues tell us it was always fun when Tommy went on to manage Albion Rovers.

At the end of the game he would invite any press there - usually about two - into his tiny office and offer them a drink.

For some reason a whisky bottle and a vodka bottle were screwed to the wall with optics, which is how we would like our office to be.

WE mentioned the death of rock'n'roller Chuck Berry and David Watson recalls seeing him in Glasgow three times. He says: "Each concert was more chaotic than the previous. The third at the Apollo saw Chuck sing the first three numbers without his guitar being plugged in. This was corrected once he eventually understood the collective baying of the audience.

"On then breaking a string and gesturing seemingly forever for a replacement, a poor wee helper was despatched on stage carrying a new string still in its packet. Chuck verbally gave the unfortunate both barrels which resulted in a replacement instrument being quickly rendered which then had to be tuned."

READERS are still reminiscing about the late Lisbon Lion Tommy Gemmell. Jim Friel recalls being in the Ballieston pub owned by Celtic star John Hughes, when Tommy was manager of Albion Rovers, whose owner Tom Fagan knew every dodge to save money.

Says Jim: "Tommy drops in to see John, and an Albion Rovers fan further up the bar pitched in with, 'I hear your jacket's oan a shaky nail down at Cliftonhill.' Tommy disagrees and tells the fan, 'We've been on a good wee run just now.' "'That's the point,' says the fan, 'Tom Fagan's no happy with all those win bonuses he's having to pay out'."

DAVID Martin recalls Tommy's great shot that scored a goal in the Lisbon final. David was with work colleagues in the Invergowrie Inn for lunch when one of them asked the three gents at the next table if they could move their table forward a little. "What are you looking for?" one asked.

"Nothing really," said his colleague. "I just wanted to see that foot again," as it was indeed Tommy Gemmell who was sitting there.

FOOTBALL fans are still talking about the sad death of Lisbon Lion Tommy Gemmell. As Jim White in Shawlands recalls: "Tommy was my hero. As a wee boy, I was taken by my dad to the boys' enclosure at Parkhead. I was standing right at the front as the ball trundled out of play towards me.

"I held it excitedly as Tommy ran over and took it from me. In the next few seconds, to motivate his teammates, he let fly more sweary words than I had ever heard in my life.

"I remember being profoundly shocked that a footballer would use such language. Ah, the innocence of youth."

AND writer Meg Henderson recalled: "Tommy was a daft big laddie. The team bus arrived at Celtic Park and the players trooped off, with Tommy grabbing a pie off the supplies which had arrived to sell at half time. The powers-that-be sent someone after him, not because he'd eaten a greasy pie just before a match, but because he hadn't paid for it."

LABOUR MP Gerald Kaufman, who has died, was a great film fan. We liked the comment of fellow MP Chris Bryant, who said: "Very sad to hear Sir Gerald Kaufman has died. The only man to have started a speech at the Parliamentary Labour Party with 'As Bette Davis once said to me ...'"

GOODNESS, that's a name from the past. A letter in *The Herald* yesterday recalled the late Walter McCorrisken who amiably tried to claim the title as Scotland's worst poet. Was it not Walter who wrote: "If it wisnae for Venetian blinds A great tragedy would befall. If it wisnae for Venetian blinds It wid be curtains for us all."

WE don't want to trespass onto Letters Page land where the poetry of the late Walter McCorrisken is being discussed, but we would just pass on from folk artist Roy Gullane: "We did a gig with him many years ago in a club in Paisley. He had everyone in stitches with a poem he said he'd written for the guy who was taking the tickets at the door. It went something like: 'My wife is poorly Walter, in fact she's so unsteady, I have to cart her doon the sterrs tae get ma breakfast ready'."

THE Letters Pages tales of pithy poet Walter McCorrisken remind *Still Game* actor Jimmy Martin: "I appeared with him once and he was just great company. I think my favourite was: 'The belly button is a wondrous thing, Of this it must be said. It's very handy for keeping salt, When you're eating chips in bed'."

THE great British comedy writer Alan Simpson of Galton and Simpson fame has died. He once explained that, when he and Ray Galton started out after meeting in a TB sanatorium, nobody knew what scriptwriters were. Said Alan: "When we went to open a bank account, the manager said, 'Well, what do you do?' and we said, 'We're scriptwriters', and he thought we did sign-writing on windows. We said, 'No, we write scripts', and he said, 'Yes, but what do you do during the day?'"

WE mentioned the sad death of the redoubtable Tam Dalyell, and former colleague Dennis Canavan recalls: "As a young teacher at Bo'ness Academy, Tam was initially given a hard time by some of the rougher elements who did not quite take to his Old Etonian style. Tam later escaped to get a job on the school ship Dunera as Deputy Director of Studies with responsibility for discipline. This led to the yarn that his former pupils at Bo'ness were reluctant to come on board, in case Tam took revenge by making them walk the plank."

AND our old chum Alistair Nicol, formerly deputy editor of the *Lothian Courier*, recalled: "Tam was a truly hard-working, highly principled MP. On one occasion I joined him on the official opening of new housing in Broxburn. One of the new residents complained of leaks from the roof so Tam borrowed a set of ladders from the construction site next door and climbed up to inspect the gutters. Suddenly, a foreman appeared and demanded to know what he was up to. 'I'm the MP for West Lothian,' he declared from on high.

"'I don't care if you're the Queen of Sheba, get aff ma f******
ladders!' was the reply."

WE will miss that fine politician and gentleman Tam Dalyell, who explained in his autobiography, *The Importance Of Being Awkward*, that within days of being elected as MP for West Lothian, he mentioned to a local newspaper editor that some Linlithgow residents had complained to him about dog mess in the streets.

The newspaper printed a story about it, and Tam was immediately phoned by the local councillor. Tam wrote: "'Tam', he said, 'Westminster, your business. Dog s***, mine'. Whereupon the telephone was slammed down. That was the first and only occasion I had a brush with West Lothian Council."

NEWS of the death of the actor Robert Hardy reminded Norrie Christie of his own time as an extra in a BBC TV film, *Between the Covers*, in which Hardy took the lead role as a writer. Norrie was in a room with fellow extras when Hardy and the director walked in and cast their gaze over them. Pointing to Norrie, the director asked if he would stand up. He did so, thinking he was about to play a scene with Hardy, but the director simply asked "Are you wearing a belt?" Norrie said he was, and was asked if Hardy could borrow it. Afterwards, when Hardy returned the belt, Norrie asked if he would kindly sign it for him. With a smile he wrote: "Thanks for the supporting role. Robert Hardy".

SAD to hear of the death of retired High Court judge Lord McCluskey who spent many years as head of the judging panel for the Scottish Press Awards.

One year he was due to make the introductory speech at the awards but was delayed by the late running of a major trial.

The then *Herald* editor Arnold Kemp was announced as the stand-in speaker but just before he stood up, Lord McCluskey arrived and told guests: "Apologies for the late arrival, and my thanks to Arnold for agreeing to step in. However I've had a glance at his speech notes and, ladies and gentlemen, you've had a lucky escape."

TV presenter Brian Cant, voice of Trumpton and presenter of *Play School*, has died. He once explained that he got the *Play School* job after turning up for an interview and he was asked to row a cardboard box. He not only rowed it, but gave a running commentary about the seagulls, the sea getting choppy, and catching a custard-filled Welly boot with his fishing rod. He reckoned he was the only person who got a job because of custard in a Wellington.

CORONATION Street regular Roy Barraclough who played shifty landlord Alec Gilroy has sadly died. We remember our journalist chum Tam Cowan once asking who was the most mentioned character on *Corrie* who never actually appeared in person.
    We were stumped until Tam told us: "Willie Ekkerslike."

SAD to hear of the death of former *James Bond* actor Sir Roger Moore. When he appeared in Glasgow recently colleague Brian Beacom asked him, if he was careful with his money, how he felt parting with the £10 million divorce cheque he reportedly wrote out to third wife Luisa Mattioli.
    "What?" he exclaimed. "I never wrote a cheque for that amount. My hand would have seized up in a cramp!" Brian also asked the secret to looking great. "Good life, good wife," said Roger, before adding: "And only ever one at a time."

THE *Herald*'s archive picture of famous Burns speaker, the Rev James Currie, reminds Eric Hudson in Bearsden: "In one Immortal Memory he told of taking his car to a garage for a service - the Burns connection evades me! - and he said to the mechanic, 'Don't charge me too much, I'm just a poor minister'. The mechanic replied, 'Aye, ah ken. I heard you on Sunday'."

MORE on the late Rev James Currie as a reader recalls that Jimmy would write down all the jokes he heard from other speakers at events he was at. Thus Jimmy Logan turned to him at one Burns Supper and asked: "Am I speaking slowly enough for you, Jimmy?" And we remember that Rikki Fulton was also amused by Jimmy's note-taking and dubbed him "The Thief of Bad Gags".

SAD to hear of the death of Sandy Strang, cricketer, and well-loved former depute rector at Hutchie, who went on to become a fine after-dinner speaker. We recall Sandy at a cricket awards dinner telling guests the difference between Saudi Arabia and Paisley's challenging Ferguslie Park housing scheme. "In Saudi Arabia," said Sandy, "you get stoned if you fornicate. In Ferguslie Park, it's the other way round."

SIR Arnold Clark who was always good company at any charity dinner I saw him at, has died. A reader once told us: "Arnold himself once served me at a dealership on Paisley Road - I think he still liked to keep his hand in. I didn't see anything I liked and went to the next dealership which, of course, was another Arnold Clark garage.

"As I was talking to the salesman Arnold himself appeared as he must have been touring all his places. He saw me and said, 'Nice to see you again'. The salesman asked if I knew Mr Clark and I quickly replied that of course I did, and what kind of deal could he offer me on the car I was looking at."

WE mentioned the sad death of outstanding teacher Sandy Strang, and former pupil Graham Richmond recalled: "In fourth year we were reading Macbeth out loud when a draught blew open the classroom door. Without cracking a light, Sandy uttered 'Enter Banquo' and then carried on as if he hadn't said a word."

WE liked when Richard Shelton appeared at the Edinburgh Fringe with his show *Sinatra and Me* telling us that he appeared in a chat show to talk about his stage appearance while wearing a tuxedo that actually belonged to Frank Sinatra.

Roger Moore, also appearing on the chat show, asked to see the label on the jacket, then said: "Yes it's Frank's. I sent him to my tailor Cyril on Saville Row after he admired mine."

OUR tales of the late Rev James Currie's storytelling remind Brian Donohoe: "One of the best I heard my friend James tell was about getting into Heaven and having to climb the stairs to the Pearly Gates where there was a blackboard to write down your sins on Earth.

"A wee guy was going back down the stairs and when asked where he was going said, 'I'm going for more chalk'."

SAD to hear of the death of *Blue Peter* presenter John Noakes, who had our nerves jangling when he climbed a ladder to the top of Nelson's Column with no safety gear.

He was so high up he later joked in an interview: "I thought I saw somebody in Glasgow waving."

WHAT a striking portrait of the late Margo MacDonald by Gerard Burns unveiled by her husband Jim Sillars at the Scottish Parliament yesterday. Scotland still misses Margo's sharp humour. We remember in her lengthy campaign to have assisted suicide legally recognised, a journalist asked if it could lead to Scotland becoming a destination for "death tourism".

"We already have it," replied Margo.

"It's called Saltcoats."

THE memorial service to Sir Terry Wogan next week reminds James Simpson in Erskine: "Terry would give a tip for a horse running that day on his radio show called Wogan's Winners. As very few tips ever came good, it was later pulled.

"Soon after, Terry was on-air reading a long-winded letter from a disgruntled listener who was explaining he had won a fortune on Wogan's Winners and had been able to build a house, take holidays, and buy a car from the proceeds. He ended the letter by demanding a reinstatement of Wogan's Winners and signed off, 'Yours Sincerely, William Hill'."

22

A Sporting Chance

Football has always been an important part of life in Glasgow, but our sporting tales have spread to other pursuits as well.

GOSH. Lots of stories about wayward Rangers player Joey Barton and claims he is being investigated for betting on football matches. As online betting firm McBookie commented: "Let's hope he didn't back himself at 8/1 to win Scottish Premiership player of the year."

TENNIS star Andy Murray has had a great few days in Glasgow, first with the Davis Cup and then with a charity invitation match. He was interviewed by some school pupils at the court with one asking if his mum Judy got upset with him occasionally swearing on court. Andy turned to see if Judy was in earshot before replying: "It was my mum I picked it up from."

CONGRATULATIONS on St Mirren recording their first league win of the season. As their fan Chris Brookmyre, the award-winning novelist mourned: "I managed to write a novel between St Mirren's last two league wins."

WE'VE not mentioned clever terracing chants for a while. Elliot Owens tells us that on Saturday in the English National League, Dagenham were playing at Forest Green where the home supporters gathered behind the goal of Dagenham keeper Elliot Justham, and kept on chanting: "You're just a crap Tesco sandwich."

SUPPORTERS' buses continued. Recalls entertainer Andy Cameron: "Was talking to a pal and he reminded me of a trip to see Rangers play Wolverhampton Wanderers in 1961. Having left Ru'glen at 6am, and drink being taken, four of us went to see Elvis in Flaming Star when we arrived early. We were then ejected for snoring.

"Mind you, if the manager hadn't put us out we would've missed the kick-off."

A CHAP in an Ayrshire golf club was telling his pals that, when he got a hole-in-one, he went home and told his wife: "I think that's my greatest ever achievement."

When she replied: "What about your three children?" he only realised later he had totally missed her point as he told her: "You're right. I should phone and tell them."

AS we read about the millions of pounds spent on footballers in England, we turn to the Scottish Juniors for some light relief. Graham Scott was at the Auchinleck Talbot v Beith game the other day when an Auchinleck fan, frustrated by a delay in the game, shouted: "C'mon ref, ah've ma work to get up for in the morning."

A Beith fan immediately shouted over: "You don't live in Auchinleck then?"

LOVELY day in Glasgow yesterday for cycling's Tour of Britain, which started in George Square with the cyclists pedalling up vertiginous Montrose Street past Strathclyde Yoonie before heading to Ayrshire. We liked the university announcing on social media: "We knew that hill would come in handy one day."

It was unkind though of another observer to comment: "Sprinting through Kilmarnock is advisable - to make sure they don't nick a bike."

CONCERNS about Partick Thistle being bottom - temporarily we hope - of the SPFL remind John Sword: "At a cold wet midweek game at Firhill in November some years ago, I heard a fan, as Thistle were losing three-nil, ask his pal, 'How long to go?' 'Another six months', he replied."

THE just-published cricket book *Test of Character* includes the tale from former Australian captain Ian Chappell of playing at Sydney Cricket Ground when he looked up and saw a spectator returning to the hill with a tray of beers. Said Ian: "He had no idea where his mates were sitting. One of them jumped up and waved and said, 'Hey Bill!' and what seemed like everyone on the hill then jumped up and yelled 'Hey Bill!' It was so spontaneous."

OUR Ayrshire golf club story reminds Robin Gilmour in Milngavie: "Some years ago before electric trolleys, a retired Procurator Fiscal for Kilmarnock had Old Sam caddying for him at an Ayrshire course. 'Well Sam!' said the Fiscal, 'I believe you were caddying for Sheriff Dickson last week. How did you get on?' '"He was rubbish Sur!', came the reply. 'He's definitely no better than yersel'".

NOT exactly a terracing shout but Bill Lothian tells us about a friend refereeing an Ayrshire junior match when he was alerted to a commotion in the away-team penalty box where home fans were pelting the goalkeeper with bread.

Explains Bill: "He couldn't work out what that was about until, a minute later, the seagulls started to swoop for the bread just as the keeper was off his line trying to cut out a cross ball amidst flurries of feathers.

"Clever these Ayrshire junior fans."

TERRACING shouts continued. Says Paul McElhone in Beckenham: "Celtic midfielder Alan Thompson impressed to such an extent that suggestions were made that he should be capped by England, and the then England manager, Sven-Goran Eriksson, made his way to the east end to watch the man himself.

"Within the opening five minutes, Thompson's first touch of the ball skittered off his foot and in all likelihood ended up bouncing its way down London Road.

"A shout was heard in the stand, 'Taxi for Ericsson!'"

OTHER sports have their wits in the stands, too.

Says David Stubley: "Not that I wish to suggest that rugby supporters are more polite than football fans, but at a premiership match at Millbrae, Ayr, a fan was heard to shout, 'Referee, your social habits are affecting your eyesight!' "I'm sure it was just helpful medical advice."

CONGRATULATIONS to Andy Murray becoming No 1 tennis player in the world. Confesses reader Gordon Shepherd: "Think I've been watching too much tennis. My wife sent me to pick up some Golden Delicious apples in the supermarket. I pick up four and by the time I get back to the trolley I've thrown two behind me and put one in my pocket."

STORIES of tough landladies remind Gordon Cubie: "The former manageress of the Premier Snooker Hall in Sauchiehall Street was one such lady. One player started whistling to himself and was immediately rebuked with, 'This is a snooker hall - not a music hall!'"

OUR tales of landladies remind Robin Gilmour: "There was the

Open Championship story of the press being tipped off that an American professional with an eye for the ladies was staying in a guest house in St Andrews.

"A reporter asked if the golfer was staying there with his wife and was told by the landlady, 'I don't think so somehow'. "When he asked why she was sure, she replied, 'Because she has a very strong Methil accent', and shut the door."

CLASSIC Scottish play *The Steamie* is going on a 30th anniversary tour next year, including shows at The King's in Glasgow and the Ayr Gaiety. It reminds us of Tony Roper, actor and writer of the play, appearing on the comedy show *Naked Radio* as a Celtic director taking empty bottles from the terraces to a shop for the deposits because of the club's perceived parsimony.

Days later he found a crate of empty beer bottles on his doorstep with a letter on Celtic club notepaper which said: "Here is your share of the takings".

AS bowling clubs close down for the winter, keen bowlers turn to the indoor clubs. A member of one such Glasgow establishment was heard this week declaring: "I wouldn't say that new member can talk, but there's a donkey in the gents' changing with its two hin' legs missing."

RANGERS fans were greatly amused by old-timer Clint Hill, at 38 the oldest player on the pitch, scoring a late equaliser yesterday to deny Celtic an 18th straight win. As one joked: "That was a goal he'll want to tell the grandkids about. In fact, he can do it when he visits them tomorrow."

SPORTS colleague Neil Cameron observes: "The *Evening Times* this week has the headline 'Rangers director Mike Ashley poised to slip into lingerie market'. Thank the Lord that sentence didn't end a word sooner.

VETERAN player and manager Tommy Docherty was in Glasgow the other week at a Legends of Football discussion night. John Henderson recalls when Tommy was manager of Manchester United and the boards listing the number of the player to be substituted were first used.

The Manchester United board showed number 11 and winger Gordon Hill eventually went near the dug-out and asked: "Does that 11 mean me?" Tommy, as United were losing at the time, replied: "No. The whole f****** team!"

SO Motherwell have parted company with manager Mark McGhee. As Scottish Comedy FC remarked on social media: "Mark McGhee's never been short on confidence. Interesting to see if he applies to replace himself at Motherwell."

However we somehow recall when Mark was manager at Aberdeen and was spat at by Aberdeen fans. Club owner Stewart Milne said on the telly that he admired McGhee "for taking it on the chin".

TALKING of football, the curly-headed and much-loved Celtic manager Wim Jansen, who stopped Rangers achieving 10-in-a-row and signed Henrik Larsson, was back to see Celtic beat Motherwell on Saturday.

When Wim suddenly resigned from being manager it came as quite a shock, other than to one Diary reader from Bothwell.

When we asked how he knew before the country's sports writers, he added: "He cancelled his papers last week at the local newsagents."

WE liked the story former Celtic player Tony Cascarino told in a recent interview when he recalled his wife being pregnant, and giving birth while he was playing a match. After the game he signed a few autographs, then stopped at a shop for a congratulations card before going on to the hospital. Said Tony: "I gave it to her and she threw it back at me from her hospital bed. I'd written 'Best Wishes, Tony Cascarino' as I was on autopilot from signing autographs."

PLANS have been submitted to knock down the Old College Bar on Glasgow's High Street and build yet another humdrum block of student flats. We recall when a group of Celtic players called in briefly to chat to the old regulars, with a couple of players accepting an invitation to sit down and have a game of dominoes.

We like the way such simple stories grow arms and legs as a few days later a tabloid reporter arrived and asked the barman: "So, is it true what they say? Is Chris Sutton really a member of the domino team here?"

DID you get caught up in the darts this week with Scotsman Gary Anderson in the final? As a reader once remarked: "You know you've got too much time on your hands when you spend 20 minutes wondering what your darts walk-on music would be."

Anyway, he seems a great chap Gary, and not at all a stereotypical Scotsman when he explained in a recent interview how he got into the game. Said Gary: "At the pub it was a pound for a game of pool. Money was tight. A game of darts was free. That's how we all got into it."

NORMAN Brown reports that the comedian Fred MacAulay was taking part in the Scottish Ladies' Open Pro-am event at Dundonald Links last week. On the first tee Fred announced: "I make people laugh for a living" - and proceeded to hit a horrible slice. There was utter silence in the crowd then someone was heard saying: "Ho ho ho!"

IT'S rarely a good idea to indulge in social-media banter with Sir Chris Hoy.

Someone tweeted him a photograph showing a South Eastern train that had been named after Hoy, and asked cheekily: "Hi Chris, when I grow up I'd like to have a train named after me too. Any tips?" Hoy replied by posting a picture of another train, saying, "I thought you already did?" This particular train only had one name written across it.

Virgin.

FORMER Hearts manager Ian Cathro came up with the occasional opaque musing, such as his "take away the goalposts and we are able to compete" and his "unless you control the scoreline then you aren't in control of anything".

Rival Hibs fans dubbed him, because of the geography of Hearts' ground, "The Dalry Lama".

A CELTIC fan tells us it was 20 years ago yesterday that Henrik Larsson signed for Celtic. He was a big hit with the ladies as well as male fans. We remember our old chum and colleague Tom Shields going on a chartered plane of fans to a Celtic European tie where he remarked on the number of female supporters with "Henrik's Girl" or "Henrik's Lass" on their jerseys. A fan from Nitshill then told Tom: "See since I put that Henrik Larsson poster on the bedroom ceiling, our love life has never been better."

SCOTLAND sadly beaten by England in the women's football the other night. Someone who watched the game explained to us: "The diving, the cheating, the childish behaviour - football just isn't the same without it."

TALKING about the weather, we liked the explanation by Scots golfer Russell Knox in a *New York Times* interview this week on why he took up a golf scholarship in his younger days at Jacksonville University in sunny Florida. Said Russell: "You grow up in Scotland and you're cold pretty much your whole life. So going to a school where the sun shines was my number one priority."

WE always find Junior football in Scotland cheers us up. Shettleston Juniors have sacked boss James McKenna after only 36 days in charge and before his new squad has even played a game. We liked James's sangfroid as he told the *Evening Times*: "A lot of people thought I wouldn't hack it in the Super First Division but here I am moving on to pastures new without losing a game."

IT'S the London Marathon later this month. A West End reader tells her pals: "Well folks, wish me luck! London Marathon is nearly here again. Last time I managed three hours and ten minutes. I'm going to try my hardest to beat my personal best - but I just get so bored, and end up turning over to watch something else."

LOOKING forward to former Celtic star, now football commentator, Charlie Nicholas's interview in the *Herald Magazine*. Charlie was able to confirm to interviewer Teddy Jamieson the infamous story of him tearing up a £20 note in front of a bothersome fan.

Said Charlie: "I think I was 17, 18. I shouldn't have been allowed in the pub. There was this guy giving me earache all night. 'I'm better than you. I'm better than you.'. Eventually I went into the gents and he was right at my back and he gave it to me again. So I eventually I took the £20 and said, 'Can you do this?' Then I ripped up the 20 quid and threw it on the ground and walked out. Two minutes later he came out and went to his mates and he looked a bit sheepish. My point was made and I sprinted straight back into the toilet to get the £20 note to Sellotape it up."

THERE'S something unique about Scottish football. Greenock Morton were playing a friendly against Turiff United at the weekend when the club noted on social media while describing the game: "Bob McHugh meets a Doyle cross with a header that skews wide and knocks club secretary Antonia Kerr's mum's pie out of her hand."

Minutes later the club added: "Excellent hospitality from the hosts as a Turiff United official appeared with a replacement pie free of charge."

SPORTS editor Stewart Weir was recalling the Dickson brothers from Larkhall who became professional boxers, with John having a handful of contests, and Alex, after the Los Angeles Olympics in 1984, winning a British title in the paid ranks.

Says Stewart: "Their introduction to pugilism came one Christmas morning, when Santa delivered each a pair of boxing gloves, draped over the frame of a bike - that's bike, singular. You've guessed it; the winner got the bike."

WE referred to Derek Whyte instead of Craig Whyte in the

Rangers fraud case story. In recompense, here is Derek's tale about moving from Aberdeen to Partick Thistle, where John Lambie was manager. Said Derek: "When John picked up a Lifetime Achievement Award he was asked what his greatest moment was. We, of course, expected him to say something about his work with Thistle but instead he answered, 'The first time I took Viagra'."

OUR mention of the late, great comedian Lex McLean reminds entertainer Andy Cameron: "In the early sixties I was in Green's Playhouse at a Rangers Rally when Lex and Rangers right-back Bobby Shearer stopped next to my seat to shoot the breeze. A wee Glasgow wummin demanded of Bobby, 'Hey you, lift up your trouser legs'. He asked why and the wee wummin, who had, it's fair to say, imbibed somewhat, explained, 'Every time ma man comes in wi' a drink in him, he says ah've got legs like Bobby Shearer, an' ah want tae see whit they look like'."

WE recall a Morton friendly against Dundee when their trialist keeper let in four goals in the first half. An irate Morton fan bought two pies at half-time and threw one at the keeper while shouting: "See if you can catch this" which, to his credit, the keeper did.

One of Tayside's finest approached to see who threw the pie but the fan held up his second pie and declared: "It wisnae me. I've still got mine."

THE *Herald* archive picture of Killermont Terminus at the end of Maryhill Road, and the mention of the prestigious Glasgow

Golf Club being just up the road, reminds Chris Keegan: "I was at a wedding in the Albany Hotel many years ago where I was being talked down to by someone boasting that he was a member of Glasgow Golf Club. The late Donald McIvor, a member at Royal Troon, overheard, and told him, 'I know that one. It's one of the better clubs in Maryhill'."

SEEMINGLY football fans in England are not impressed by the quality of football north of the Border. A reader in London tells us he was in his local on Sunday when a toper watching the Sky Sports News remarked: "Seeing all the Celtic fans celebrating winning the Scottish Premiership reminds me of the time when I broke out the champagne after beating my six-year-old daughter at arm wrestling."

FORMER Rangers player Joey Barton is back in the news over bets on matches. Asks John Henderson: "I see he has been suspended with immediate effect from all football activity for 18 months. Does this mean he's free to rejoin the Rangers midfield?" And James Martin declares: "Joey Barton said to be devastated about 18-month ban from football for gambling, as he had £20 on it being two years."

IT'S the Grand National tomorrow and we remember the year Mon Mome won and a disgruntled punter in a Glasgow bookie's declared: "A 100/1 shot winning the National. What are the odds of that?"

SUNDERLAND'S Glaswegian manager David Moyes is in

trouble for joking with a female spots reporter that she "would get a slap". It reminds us of when he took over as manager of Manchester United, and was less than convincing. The joke at the time was: "What's the difference between Prince Andrew and Manchester United?" The answer being: "Prince Andrew has never regretted getting rid of Fergie."

EUROMILLIONS winners Colin and Christine Weir are to build a £4m training centre which they will then lease to Partick Thistle, who have never had their own training ground. It reminds us of course of when the players were training in Ruchill Park and a couple of neds were shouting at the players. Chic Charnley told them to come back after training "for a chat", which they did with a samurai sword, a knife and a fighting dog.

Chic charged the guy with the sword wielding a traffic cone until the ned ran off.

I'm told that Chic was called to the police station but did not pick the ned out in a line-up. When asked why, he replied: "I'm frae Possil, I'm no' a grass."

LOTS of folk have been commenting on how bad golfer Tiger Woods looks in his police picture after being arrested for suspected drink-driving.

Well done to bookie Paddy Power coming to his defence by telling one critic: "No kidding? Doubt the police gave him 30 goes at it and a filter like your selfies on Instagram."

FORMER Rangers manager Dick Advocaat becoming boss of the Dutch team reminds us of former referee Willie Young often having to speak to Dick about his angry behaviour on the touch-line. Finally, before a game at Ibrox, Willie went up to Dick in the dressing room and asked him: "When shall I come over to see you, Dick?" "Sorry?" asked a bemused Advocaat.

"Should we make an appointment?" continued Willie. "You'll start jumping up and down, and I'll have to halt everything to come over and speak to you.

"Shouldn't we just arrange a time now?" The point was taken.

OUR story about the old golfer reminds Stewart Little: "I once enquired of a golfer loading his clubs into his car if he had had a good round. His reply was, 'Any round is good as long as I am this side of the grass'."